1,001
THINGS TO DO
IN SACRAMENTO
WITH KIDS

(& The Young At Heart)

1,001
THINGS TO DO
IN SACRAMENTO
WITH KIDS
(& The Young At Heart)

by
Sabrina Nishijima

Illustrated by
Sarah Golden

Sacramento, California

1,001 Things To Do In Sacramento With Kids (& The Young At Heart)
Sabrina Nishijima
Illustrated by Sarah Golden

First edition, First printing
First published in the United States in 2018 by Sactown Kids

ISBN: 978-0-692-06185-5
Nishijima, Sabrina.
1,001 things to do in Sacramento with kids (& the young at heart) / by Sabrina
Nishijima. – 1st ed.

Published by Sactown Kids
Printed in the United States by Ingram
Distributed in the United States and Worldwide by Ingram

Ingram is certified by the Forest Stewardship Council® (FSC®). The FSC® Council
is a non-profit organization, promoting the environmentally appropriate, so-
cially beneficial and economically viable management of the world's forests.
FSC® certification is recognized internationally as a rigorous environmental
and social standard for responsible forest management. FSC® Certificate Reg-
istration Code: RA-COC-004900 FSC-C084699.

SACTOWN KIDS
A SMALL PRESS PUBLISHER
Sacramento, California
www. sactownkids.com

PUBLISHER'S NOTE: The information in this book is not intended as a
substitute for calling or verifying business hours and admission information,
which can fluctuate from year to year. The places mentioned in this book may
change hours, policies, or may be undergoing construction or renovations
that may affect visiting hours. Take all necessary precautions when planning
your trip. Call ahead, abide by current laws, and participate in all activities at
your own risk. While every effort has been made to ensure the accuracy of this
guidebook, environmental conditions, availability, websites, phone numbers,
and other information can change at any time. The author and publisher do
not assume and hereby disclaim any liability to any party for any loss, damage,
or disruption caused by errors or omissions, whether such errors or omissions result from negligence, accident, or any other cause.

For my boys, Milo and Andrew,
my favorite dreamers.
NEVER STOP ADVENTURING. LIFE IS SHORT.

– S.N.

To my girls, Sadie & August.

– S.G.

TABLE OF CONTENTS

INTRODUCTION

I felt my lungs inflate with the onrush of scenery – air, mountains, trees, people. I thought, "This is what it is to be happy."

– Sylvia Plath

When I look over the railings of the golden Tower Bridge in Sacramento with my two little kids, their faces shining bright with innocence (and a touch of mystery muck), the minutia of the day and all the travails of getting there fall away. We are free. The kids are excited, full with wonder, pointing things out to me with a sense of urgency, whispering to the birds as cars whiz by. We watch the Sacramento River rush under us – riveting at first, then receding into the background – water patterns delineating to the banks where tall trees cloister squirrels that skitter up and down foraging for food. We walk lazily along the river, grab sticks, sit on the dirt on our bare pants, try to make each other laugh, skip rocks onto the water, say hello to people walking by, and watch the boats drift by. Inevitably, we spot something in the distance and decide to venture further to see what it is, and I think – this is a good day. This is the best part of life.

We love living here. "America's Farm to Fork Capital" the "City of Trees," the "Fruit Basket of America." We're right at the heart of the golden triangle that encompasses Lake Tahoe, San Francisco, and Napa--what a great place to be. Sacramento is such a diverse, dynamic, ever-changing city with new activities, restaurants, and shops popping up every week.

As parents, we're inundated with so many responsibilities, expectations, and obligations, that when we decide to set afoot somewhere new with the kids, sometimes we're just stumped. We know full well there's no shortage of things to do in this exciting city, but we simply don't have the bandwidth to keep a fresh flow of ideas in our brain at all times, or sit down at a computer and do extensive research every day.

I wrote this book so that we have a torrent of possibilities at the ready, and so that other families can also share in the same adventures and misadventures! Some of the first few dozen entries are our tried-and-true favorites, but we haven't tried most of these thousand-and-one ideas. We have some circled for this month, and we love not knowing what the future holds. Let us know what adventures you love in Sacramento--we want to know!

The entries are purposely thrown together at random to spark the imagination. Sometimes the best adventures are a riff off of what you intended to do. If an activity or location is too far away or too difficult to get to, find something similar closer to you or that fits within your family's comfort zone. Or keep a folding frisbee in your bag, and any park or open space turns into a good time.

Of course, not every day has to be a crazy, new adventure. My family loves the simplest things like biking around the same old streets in our neighborhood, pulling our beloved three-legged dog in our red wagon, going to the same swimming pool over and over (Thanks, Huong!), and waiting for it to rain so we can run around outside with our umbrellas. Simple is the best. But for those days when you look at each other and collectively yearn for something new and different – this book will be your faithful companion.

Sometimes, when I'm in the heat of the battle (i.e. dealing with multiple kid mishaps in succession, alone, with dirty pants and unwashed hair), I blindly throw clothes on the kids, get them zipped up in the car with nary a clear idea of our destination. Sometimes we wind up doing something eccentric and over-the-top, like stumbling upon an out-of-the-way Latino cultural center where we decide to sign up to build an altar for Dias de los Muertos. But sometimes – without compunction – we drop by Chuck E. Cheese, just to see if we can beat the current basketball game score. *(We can't.)*

Most of the time, we just run around outside at parks, which always seems to be just what the kids had in mind anyway. As long as we have a mini-football or scooter, we're good to go.

I've tried to feature as many outdoor nature activities as possible, because it seems to be what kids are naturally drawn to and thrive on. The leading scientists agree, kids crave the natural world and new experiences. Studies continue to show that the more time kids spend outdoors, the more happy and well-adjusted they are, and the better emotional regulation they have in adulthood. But we all know that intuitively. When we're outside, visiting with friends, soaking up the sunshine, running through an open field or walking hand-in-hand through a cozy forest, we feel good. Time slows down. It's the best.

As my eldest son, Milo, suggests in the last entry of this book (#1,001), kids just love playing with other kids whose imaginations are as creative and wild as their own. To him, it doesn't matter where he is, he just loves to play with kids. Even in a constrained adult world, kids feel like anything is possible when they're with other kids. Recently, we went to the Indian Grinding Rock State Historic Park (#384) with some new friends, and next to the wide grassy field, a large fallen tree sat with a hole in its trunk, just wide enough for small bodies to climb through. The infinite possibilities of play represented by this one fallen tree and its cavernous hideout was a dream come true for the kids, who delighted in climbing all over it.

To be fair, my youngest son, Andrew, a toddler, was unable to contribute to this book, but I watch him at his happiest making a mess at Art Beast, and chasing little friends at Bertha Henschel Park's playground who, most of the time, are perfectly unaware that they are being chased. But a short hike (1/4th mile) or walk through a wooded area is a feast for his senses, and lucky for us we live in the one of the most tree-dense cities in the world (just Singapore and Vancouver, Canada beat out Sacramento).

My husband, Daniel, contributed so many ideas to this book, and I often researched ideas specifically with him in mind, as he venerates the new and unusual. His favorite things to do with the kids run the gamut from getting food samples at Costco, to getting haircuts, to going to farm-to-fork dinners at Full Belly Farm (#99) – which might be our new favorite thing to do with our friends (Thanks, Ravi!).

While this book is geared toward kids and teens, I searched high and low and journeyed far down rabbit holes to discover new ideas that everyone would enjoy, no matter what their age. The thirst for daily adventure is something most people don't outgrow, no matter what their age.

A mother-friend once told me, "I feel like most of my job as a mother is just getting my kids outside to play and try new things." and I couldn't agree more (Thanks, Helen!). This is the life purpose I feel most *people* have, not just parents, and I hope this book fulfills its promise to inspire new and exciting adventures in Sacramento and beyond.

A special thanks to Sarah Golden, the incredible and prolific artist and mother who collaborated with me on this book. Without her wild imagination, you may not have started reading.

From our families to yours – Happy Adventuring!

xo, Sabrina

1,001

1   Blow some crazy, **giant bubbles at Capitol Park** and
    then drink a fresh, hand-pounded berry lemonade
    across the street at **Cafeteria 15L**.

2   **Rent a kayak, hydrobike, canoe, paddle board, or
    paddle boat** at **Sacramento State Aquatic Center**
    at Lake Natoma. Adults can take a 14-hour sailing
    course and then rent sailboats for the family. Yes, you
    can do it.

3   Find the milky way and see planets up-close, year-
    round at Folsom Lake College's free **Community
    Observatory** in Placerville, away from the city
    lights. Friendly and knowledgeable docents are
    always on-hand for brief talks and Q&A's. Brilliant
    astronomy students help set-up telescopes for some
    awe-inspiring night viewing. A new imaging dome
    allows for specialized "deep space" viewings. Every
    Friday, Saturday, and Sunday nights at 8:30pm, or
    7:30pm in the winter. Always check online calendar
    before going. Cancellations because of weather are
    made at least 60 minutes ahead of scheduled events.
    communityobservatory.com

4   Jump into the pristine **Jenkinson Lake**, an hour away
    at the Sly Park Recreation Area. Park in the day use
    area near site #15 and #16 to swim across a shallow
    isthmus to a tiny island that's fun to explore.

5   **Walk across Tower Bridge** an hour before sunset, when it's saturated in all its golden glory.

6   Spend the afternoon discovering new art and photography exhibits at **Crocker Art Museum**, and grab a popsicle from Crocker Café to enjoy in the park across the street on your way out. The cute, little Tot Land children's space features a large, wooden play boat and reading nook. Wee Wednesdays gallery program for ages 3-5 is free with admission. Admission to the museum is $10 adults, free for kids 6 & under.

7   Book a free **swan tour** November through January and watch thousands of beautiful Tundra swans migrating to sunny California for the winter, across privately owned rice fields and restored habitats. Naturalists are on-hand to fill you in on all the quirky details of the birds and their long journey from the remote lands of the Arctic. For older kids and teens. California Department of Fish & Wildlife. *wildlife.ca.us*

8   Get the kids centered with Midtown Yoga's (MiYo) **Free Yoga at Fremont Park** at P & 16th. Wiggly kids welcome. Tuesdays and Thursdays 6pm-7pm through Sept, subject to change. Arrive 10 minutes early for check-in. Bring a mat or towel and water.

9   Average annual precipitation in Sacramento is just 18 inches. Relish the rare rainy days! Slip on your rubber boots and **splash in puddles** in your favorite Sacramento neighborhood. Don't forget to take a towel in the car to sit on for the drive home.

10   Bug out at the **Bohart Museum of Entomology at UC Davis**, the **seventh largest insect collection in North America**. It also functions as a working lab, so there's a chance you can catch a scientist sorting rare wasps or butterflies – they'll be happy to answer questions. Check their calendar for family-friendly open house events. Don't miss the newly discovered moth species named after Donald Trump, or *neopalpa donaldtrump*. According to the entomologist, "The reason for this choice of name is to bring wider public attention to the need to continue protecting fragile habitats in the US that still contain many undescribed species. The specific epithet is selected because of the resemblance of the scales on the frons (head) of the moth to Mr. Trump's hairstyle." Free.

11   Get $10 lawn tickets for a **River Cats baseball game** and let the kids chase each other up and down the gentle slope. Kids can run the bases on Sunday Fundays. Catch some fireworks after Saturday games, or $1 hot dogs and ice cream cups on Family Value Tuesdays.

12   Spiral down the tree house slide and **walk along the Crooked Mile** at Fairytale Town.

13   Discover how to play the **ukulele, hula dance, or thread flowers into a lei** at the annual **Sacramento Aloha Festival** in October. Visit the "keiki" (kids) corner, and eat some "ono" (good) food. Don't forget the shaved ice!

14   Go on the popular **bat tour** in the Yolo Bypass Wildlife Area between Sacramento and Davis, June through September, with the Yolo Basin Foundation, and meet the largest colony of Mexican Free-Tailed bats in California. Bat Talks & Walks, $12 adults, kids 15 & under free. Must reserve far in advance, and they sell out quickly – so get on their newsletter list.

15   Spend the morning at **Art Beast Children's Studio** on K St. making new daily craft projects, playing with freshly made play dough, "baking" some pies in the outdoor kitchen, trying on some costumes, or taking a music class. Designed for kids under 7. Proceeds benefit the Tubman House, a non-profit program that helps teen mothers in need. Bring a lunch or snacks for the kids – they won't want to leave.

16   Climb aboard a high-speed rail simulator, a real steam locomotive, and play with toy trains at the **California Railroad Museum.** Don't miss All Aboard Storytime Mondays at 11am in the East Theater.

17   **Be brave and sing karaoke** at a family-friendly place like **Oishii Sushi & Karaoke Bar**. Go early (usually 4-6pm) for half-off karaoke rooms.

18   Pick up endless fascinating facts on trees, raptors, lizards, and coyotes at **Effie Yeaw Sacramento Nature Center** a 100-acre nature preserve in Carmichael. Hit up their nice, easy, flat trails on any day of the week and you're guaranteed to see some deer, birds, bugs, and wild turkeys. Find out when their next nature walk is being held, and take a hike down to the river or through the forest with a naturalist. Trails are open dawn to dusk. Nature Center building is open February-October. Parking is $5, sometimes free for special events, call ahead.

19   See a family-friendly, world-class theatre production at the **Harris Center for Performing Arts**. Find a musical by **El Dorado Musical Theatre**, a group of youth performers who are simply out-of-this-world.

20   **Volunteer for the Special Olympics** Northern California events, and work with extraordinary kid athletes in 11 sports in Sacramento. Kids ages 10 & up can become volunteers. Kids ages 14 & up can coach!

21   Explore the area around **Lake Clementine's waterfall** dam to get loaded up on positivity-inducing negative ions. Bring some fresh-squeezed orange juice and snacks. Explore the area.

22   Rent the **2.5" button maker** at the Arcade Public
      Library's "Library of Things" and punch your own
      button designs for fun or make a treasured gift.

23   Go to Vierra Farms in West Sacramento and try the
      ultra-sweet **Black Imagination Watermelons** –
      which many people agree are the best-tasting
      watermelon on earth. Get three varieties of
      watermelons and have a blind taste test at home to see
      if you can identify each one.

24   Make and eat some homebaked tator tots (or other
      favorite snack) in the **World Peace International
      Rose Garden** at the Capitol. Pick your favorite rose
      and take a picture in front of it.

25   Put on your 'science eyes' and wander the 1-mile
      Nature Trail through beautiful oak woodlands at
      Placer Nature Center. Eat a picnic in the garden
      afterwards, where you can learn about different types
      of composting methods in action. Play hide & seek in
      the Native American Village. A Watershed learning
      exhibit inside the museum details the life cycle of a
      single drop of water, and tells us what we can do to
      protect this precious natural resource. Don't miss the
      giant, topographic map of Placer County.

26   **Eat outside in a storm.** The Flower Farm Café's
      enclosed outdoor heated porch is open even in a
      downpour of rain. Discover the magic of a rainy day.

27   Stop to **do some good**. Pick up an extra bag of oranges or apples at a farmer's market and offer them to people in need on your way home, or at a city park like Cesar Chavez Plaza on J St.

28   Eat food from Punjab, India and celebrate with thousands of Sikhs at Yuba City's annual **Sikh Parade Festival** every November. The first Sikh pioneers came here more than 110 years ago, and their religion teaches that all races and faiths are equal.

29   Go to a **baby or toddler storytime** at a Sacramento Public Library. Stay and play with soft toys and trade funny parenting fails other careworn parents. It's always fun to venture out to a new neighborhood and meet new friends and librarians.

30   Push scarves into a see-through air tunnel, play mailman, and make a topographic map change by moving sand around with your hands at the **Sacramento Children's Museum**. Constantly evolving exhibits and toddler events keep things fresh. A baby area with lots of padding is perfect for crawlers. Ages 8 & under.

31   Visit the Downtown Ice Rink November through January for some **magical, outdoor ice skating** at Rose of Lima Park on K Street. Especially magical at night. $6 for kids 6 & under.

32 Sit under the stars, **roast marshmallows and listen to native Maidu stories** around the campfire. Every 3rd Friday, April through October, 7-8:30pm, at the **Maidu Museum & Historic Site** in Roseville. $5/person, $16/family of four, 2 & under free.

33 **Watch a sloth** move ever so slowly at the **Sacramento Zoo**. Then memorize the differences between a Masai and Reticulated giraffe, and find out why their tongues are black. Don't miss the Wildlife Stage Shows in the amphitheater at 11am, where you can pet some of the animals after the show. Look up when Keeper Chats are occurring at various locations within the zoo, and learn more about your favorite animals. There's also an animal hospital where you can watch veterinarian exams through large glass windows every morning, except Wednesdays. The animal doctor dictates some of the live action for visitors who stop by.

34 **Ride a carousel powered by human pedalers** volunteering for a good cause in the summer at **Davis Farmer's Market** at Davis Central Park on Wednesday nights, 4:30pm - 8:30pm. Eat an early homemade picnic dinner and enjoy the bounce houses until it gets dark.

35 **Climb into a Model T**, one of the first cars built for mass consumption at the **California Automobile Museum**. Yes, they actually let kids climb into a few vintage cars! Wear green on St. Patrick's Day, or your Halloween costume on Halloween, and get in for half-price. Take a Youth Basic Engine class and take apart a Briggs & Stratton one cylinder engine to see how the solids, liquids, and gases interact. Or take Racing & Engineering for Teens.

36 Jump into the flight simulator at the **Aerospace Museum of California**. Then, walk around outside and see more than 50 different types of aircrafts, several of which are open each day, weather permitting. Don't miss the Top Gun 'F-14' Tomcat. Open Cockpit Events takes place twice annually. Be sure to talk to the former pilots and aviation experts now serving as volunteer docents – they are walking encyclopedias on everything aviation-related. Little ones will have fun exploring the Kids Zone on the 2nd floor.

37 **Create a family altar** for **Dia de los Muertos** (Day of the Dead) celebrating love, life, and your departed loved ones for the annual **El Panteón de Sacramento** in Midtown. Any person or family can reserve a space for $25 and take part in the magical celebration. Usually held at the end of October every year. Be sure to bring the kids at night for live music and a festive celebration!

38   Flip over some **new gymnastics tricks** at a trial
class at your nearest gymnastics gym, like Planet
Gymnastics, Fliptastic!, Byers, Youngsters Inc.,
International Gymnastics Centre, Rega, SET
Gymnastics, Fliptastic, Tumblebuddies, etc.
Sacramento loves gymnastics!

39   File a permit with the County to **place a geocache
box in your favorite public park.** Have fun with
your "outdoor scavenger hunt" at *geocaching.com.*

40   Drive to **Bluestone Meadow Lavender Farm** in
Placerville to see the lavender bloom in the soft
morning or afternoon light during the summer.
They grow more than twenty different varieties. Kids
can run through the fields and cut their own fresh
lavender mid-June to mid-July. Let the older kids
create their own lavender wreaths, sachets, or wands.
Staff is on-hand for to provide instructions and
supplies. They are also open on weekends in October.

41   View **Sacramento's skyline** from the 16th floor of
the Robert T. Matsui Courthouse at 501 I St. A floor-
to-ceiling glass window and public viewing area gives
kids ample viewability to search for landmarks like
the Sacramento River, Tower Bridge, Golden1 Center,
and the Wells Fargo building, the tallest building
downtown. There are couches to sit on and sculptures
to enjoy. No cameras are allowed in the building, but
they do let you keep your smartphone, *wink-wink.*

42   Take a trip to **Sutter's Fort State Historic Park** in Midtown and **get transported to the wild, lawless pioneer world** of the early 1800s. Sutter's Fort was the earliest settlement in California's Central Valley, and John Sutter's life story is fascinating. Then, get some fancy house-made lemonade at **Paragary's** ($4) on 28th St., just three blocks away.

43   Visit the tiny **3.5-acre Charles C. Jensen Botanical Park** in Carmichael and run across a mini-bridge over a babbling creek. Walk through the 200 species of camellias, azaleas, and rhododendrons. Try to count the eight different types of dogwood trees. Print the plant & tree identification document before going: *http://carmichaelpark.com/jensen-botanical-garden/*

44   Eat your way to better health at the kid-friendly **Sactown Vegfest** in January, eat some vegan gelato, and stop by the Kids Zone.

45   See **salmon jumping up the fish ladders** in November and December at the **Nimbus Fish Hatchery**. Visit the museum inside and see through the head of a salmon fish. Bring quarters to feed the thousands of fish in the outdoor fish rearing ponds.

46   Pick up some mouthwatering, **kid-friendly, low-sugar, gluten-free cupcakes and desserts** for your friends at Pushkin's Bakery on 29th St., or Pushkin's Restaurant, the gorgeous and modern location on Capitol Ave.

47   Visit a **new park you've never been to** and explore what another Sacramento neighborhood has to offer. There are **226 parks** in the city of Sacramento! *http://www.cityofsacramento.org/ParksandRec/Parks/Park-Directory*

48   Pick up the fabulous book **The California Naturalist Handbook** by the University of California Press, and read a new page every day. Teach the kids about the Sacramento Valley's geology, native animals and plants, freshwater resources and ecosystems, and so much more. You'll become an active 'citizen scientist' in no time! Start a nature journal for all your strange and cool observations and discoveries.

49   Visit the **Aggie Reuse Store at UC Davis**, where students divert materials from winding up in landfills and redistribute them at low cost for reuse and re-purposing! You'll get a first-hand look at the creative, modern work of young design students. TB 24, University of California, One, Shields Ave, Davis, CA. Hours are very limited, so call and plan ahead.

50   Listen to traditional, artistic religious music performed *a cappella* by a local group like the **Vocal Art Ensemble**, and listen to happiness-inducing colorful harmonies

51   Go to a **planetarium show** at the Powerhouse Science Center. Saturdays and Sundays 1pm & 3pm. Ages 4 & up.

52   **Arrange a local radio station tour** and see what goes on behind-the-scenes when they're live, on-air. Studio tours can be arranged with the following stations: 106.5 KUDL, 1320 KIFM, 107.9 KDND, 94.7 KKDO, 98.5 KRXQ, and 96.9 KSEG. NPR doesn't do individual family tours at this time, but can sometimes arrange a group tour. Contact their Community Relations Department.

53   **Feed the 40+ beautiful Koi fish i**n the Japanese ponds for 25-cents at Fairytale Town. Look for the machines with the fish food next to the Japanese ponds.

54   Get your winter shoes on and **walk through a snow meadow** to get to Nevada Beach at Zephyr Cove, Lake Tahoe. It's a kid-friendly, beautiful, 1-2-mile flat hike.

55   **Take the light rail** to a destination nearby, like
      Historic Folsom. Jump on the Gold Line on 16th
      St. for a fun, one-hour train ride. Plan ahead and
      coincide your trip with a special event taking place.
      Kids with student I.D. pay just $1.25.

56   **Slide on a flattened cardboard box** at Slide Hill
      Park in Davis. Wear old pants or jeans that need a little
      more ripping. Try to out-slide the kids, and wear your
      bravery loud and proud.

57   Make a simple **DIY sewing or knitting project** in
      a crafting class at Jo-Ann Fabric & Craft Stores. For
      crafters 8 & up.

58   Throw some lawn chairs in the car, and **watch the
      unforgettable sunset** from the Yolo Bypass between
      Sacramento and Davis. Bring some takeout tacos and
      horchata and make it a special event to remember. For
      some memorable tacos, try La Venadita or Chando's.

59   Meet 30 inspiring painters, photographers,
      ceramicists, and jewelry artisans at **Panama Art
      Factory's** next open house.

60   Pop in to **Danny's Mini Donuts** in Old Sacramento
      for the miniature version of your favorite donuts.
      Made fresh on-site, daily.

61   Wander through a cluster of art galleries on the
Second Saturday Art Walks, 4pm - 9pm. Some good
bets are R St. between 10th & 13th St., 20th & 21st
Streets between I & J St., Verge Center for the Arts at
625 S St. Find a complete list of galleries and some art
previews: *2ndsaturdaysacramento.com*

62   Go to Mace Ranch Park in Davis and find the
"Evidence of Life" solar calendar. Sit on the center
stone. The peripheral stones mark where we can look
to observe the sunrise and sunset at the first day of
each season: the spring equinox, the summer solstice,
the fall equinox, and the winter solstice.

63   Attend a **Save-a-Life Saturday** with the American
Red Cross, where kids and adults of all ages can learn
life-saving skills, like hands-only CPR.

64   Watch an **exciting high school or college
sports game** and cheer on our home teams, like
the Sacramento State Hornets, UC Davis Aggies,
American River College Beavers, and the Sacramento
City College Panthers.

65   Take a **free trial class at Sacramento Water Polo's**
year-round youth program, and put your swimming
skills to the test. Ages 8-14. Practices and scrimmages
are at Sierra College. Check their calendar and watch a
competitive youth game.

66   Watch the makings of millions of jelly bellies on the 1/4th-mile **self-guided factory tour of Jelly Belly** in Fairfield. Exhibits and games are placed along the tour, as well as free samples. Skip the long lines with the Chocolate & Wine Experience for $20. Kids OK.

67   Join a youth volleyball team and learn how to serve, cover, dink, and spike. **West Sacramento Youth Volleyball** league meets in the spring at Bryte Park. Ages 7-15.

68   Got your own snow sled or inflatable tube? Get a **SNO-PARK** pass for $25 and enjoy unlimited play at 19 public snow park sites maintained by the Department of Parks and Recreation from November 1st through May 30th. Always bring snow chains and a shovel.

69   Celebrate the world's cultures and take in the colorful sights, costumes, music, and dancing at the annual **Elk Grove Multicultural Festival** in August. Free parking and admission.

70   Support local **professional ballet companies** and get ready to be wowed by their next performance. Local favorites include Sacramento Ballet, Capitol Ballet, Sac Civic Ballet, and Pamela Hayes.

71   Set off on a raft or **rowboat at Hogback Island Access**, along the Sacramento River, and enjoy grassy picnic areas and a nice lagoon.

72   Dress up as your favorite Disney character for **Disney On Ice** at Golden 1 Center. A new themed-show comes through town at least twice a year.

73   Build a DIY project at **Home Depot's Kids Building Workshop** on Saturdays 9am - 12pm. Register before Saturdays to reserve a spot at *homedepot.com*

74   **Enter the world of scuba diving** at the Discover Scuba Diving program at Scuba World. Ages 10 & up.

75   Drop in to the **Kids Adventure Club** on Thursdays at Sunrise Mall for some free storytelling, sing-a-longs, and crafts. Register at the Customer Service desk.

76   Scream and jump all you want cheering on the **Sacramento Republic soccer** team at their home games. Face painting should be mandatory.

77   Spend a weekend day at the **"Ducks and Scopes"** event at the **Consumnes River Preserve**, where nature docents have telescopes set-up for kids and families to enjoy seeing colorful ducks, geese, and shorebirds like Black-Neck Stilts and Common Snipes. Recent table displays have featured "Duck Soup," dishes of water dipped from the pond full of sand fleas, dragonfly nymphs, and other squiggly things that provide the protein the birds feed on, with microscopes for up-close discoveries. Usually from 10am - 2pm.

78   Bring a bucket for water, and cups for molds, and **build a sand castle** at Southside Park's sandbox. Enlist the help of other sand enthusiasts.

79   Get the hang of skiing and snowboarding at the family-friendly **Planet Kids at Soda Springs Resort**. Climb a snow volcano, practice moving around in skis on a flat area, or go tubing on a gentle slope.

80   Brew up some hot chocolate in a family-size Stanley's mug and watch the **State Capitol Christmas Tree Lighting**.

81   **Watch wildflowers open up** in late spring during a family bike ride along the American River. Try to identify all the species you see. Dissect a flower with scissors and see what they look like when you cut them down the middle.

82   Catch a glimpse of Victorian life and tour the opulent **Leland Stanford Mansion**, which was the governor's office before the State Capitol was built. Recommended for older kids and teens. Limited hours.

83   Go to **Children's Book Week** at Fairytale Town in May and plop down on the grass for daily storytimes and kids' activities.

84   Get a **big shaved ice in the shape of a gnome's hat** at downtown's Osaka-Ya on 10th St.

85   In January, head over to the **Galt Winter Bird Festival** for kid-friendly presentations, talks, art activities, exhibits, and food.

86   Get your fill of singing, jumping, and puppet fun at the **Mother Goose on the Loose! Storytime** events at the Roseville public library, most weekdays 10:30 - 11am. *roseville.ca.us*

87   Tinker with creative materials in endless creative ways at the free play afterschool program, **Adventure Playground** at the Maple Neighborhood Center. Ages 7-15. *sacadventureplay.org*

88   In June, walk 1.5 miles for children battling life-threatening illnesses in the **Walk for Love** fundraiser for the Northern California Shriners Hospital for Children.

89   **Watch live folklorico dancers**, listen to Latin bands, and eat traditional Mexican cuisines at the family-friendly **Cinco de Mayo Festival** at Southside Park. Free.

90   Collaborate and pore over the fundamentals of engineering at a **Lego enrichment program at Play-Well TEKnologies**.

91   **Start a Neighborhood Watch group** on your
     street through the Sacramento County Sherriff's
     Department, and teach your kids basic crime
     prevention. Strengthen a sense of community with
     your neighbors, especially for your kids.

92   Join a **serious rock climbing team** at Rocknasium
     in Davis (ages 12-18). Kids 6 & up can join in on
     supervised Kid Climbs, where they practice agility,
     strength, and overcoming mental challenges. $35 for
     2 hours.

93   Find out when your local Sacramento elementary
     and middle schools are having their **Harvest or Fall
     Festivals in autumn** for some low-cost family-
     friendly fun. There's usually lots of fun games,
     face-painting, and live music. Most of these school
     festivals aren't advertised (except for posters in the
     neighborhood) but they welcome the public.

94   **Get a garden plot of your own** with the City of
     Sacramento Parks & Recreation and make friends
     with green thumbs. Learn about the cycle of plant life
     and the importance of composting.

95   Slip down **easy water slides with babies and
     toddlers** at Adventure Island swimming spot at
     Golfland SunSplash.

96   See the **spring bloom of wildflowers and get a waterfall rush** at Hidden Falls Regional Park in Auburn. It's a 1.5-mile hike to the falls and back, mostly uphill back. Get there before 10am on weekends, or go on a slow weekday. Parking reservations are required on weekends. *placer.ca.gov*

97   **Watch a real cider mill** make delicious, sweet, unfiltered apple cider at **Rainbow Orchards** in Apple Hill. Share one of their famous cider donuts, utilizing the fresh-pressed cider straight from their mill.

98   **Rent a ViewSonic Lightstream DLP Projector** from Sacramento Public Library's "Library of Things." Hang a white sheet in your front or backyard, throw down some blankets and pillows, and **screen a movie for the neighborhood kids** from your laptop.

99   Experience California farm-to-fork at **Full Belly Farm**, the beautiful 400-acre certified organic farm that opens its arms to visitors and families. Book ahead in winter or spring for one of their enchanting, **moonlit summer farm dinners**, April through October. A lofty, modern barn-like kitchen and outdoor dining patio sits adjacent to an expansive grassy area and apple orchards for kids to run through. Casual wood fired pizza dinners don't require reservations. Diners are welcome to **camp overnight on the farm** – just be sure to notify them in advance. I can't recommend this enough for local, farm-loving families. Bring your own wine.

100   Take part in **California Duck Days**, an annual wetlands and wildlife festival hosted by the Yolo Basin Foundation in February with tours and kids activities. Free for kids under 16.

101   Get your mark, set, and run with the **Sacramento Running Association's year-round running programs**. Ages 5 & up. Sign-ups for the Spring Track Program start in April.

102   In June, wear your rainbow gear and head down to the **Sacramento Pride Festival** on the Capitol Mall between 3rd & 4th St. for great music, performances, food, and a Kids Zone. Children 10 & under are free. The colorful Pride parade usually starts at 11am.

103   See a funny, family-friendly play at **B Street Theatre**. Plan ahead and check when the next family series starts. Their Children's Theatre of California is a professional theatre company that produces four original plays September through May.

104   Take a 4-hour beginner's **fly fishing** class in the American River with Jeff Putnam's popular fly fishing school. Discover all the secrets for tying knots, rigging, fly selection, entomology, and how to read water.

105   **Discover new children or teen books** at the **Avid Reader at Broadway Station** bookstore. Pick out a good one, and start reading it under a canopy of trees in nearby Land Park. Support our independent bookstores!

106   **Transport to India** and feast on some delicious **Indian samosas**, masalas, naan breads, and chutneys at Bombay Grill or Pooja Indian Grill. Mylapore in Folsom has great dosas, a pancake-like wrap with savory fillings.

107   Visit **The Cannery**, a farm-to-fork residential community in Davis, which has its own working farm and fun food events throughout the year. Stop by Ikeda's impeccable fruit stand on Mace Blvd. on your way home for more fresh, totally local produce.

108   Find out what the differences are between falcons, hawks, eagles and kite birds that fly Sacramento's friendly skies. Look up their **"flight silhouettes"** online and see if you can tell the difference between them the next time you spot one.

109   Get inspired to **start a family sewing project** at the colorful Annual Vintage Quilt Show at the Folsom History Museum. Each year features a new pattern theme. It's truly a feast for the eyes. Ask the quilters how many hours it takes them to make one quilt.

110   Explore the world of NASA flight missions, chemistry, robots, and the mysteries of matter with a **Mad Science** afterschool program or camp.

111   Walk or ride all or part of the **Davis-Covell Greenbelt** in Davis. This 2.7-mile loop is flat, dog-friendly, and crosses large, grassy areas. Along the way, look for cherry blossoms in spring, giant dominos, dog sculptures, and the Julie Portansky Pond at Northstar Park.

112   Soak in the hot springs at **Grover Hot Springs State Park** in Markleeville near Tahoe. The water's intense green color is caused by the mineral deposits at the bottom. There's a campground and hiking trails nearby. $10 adult, $5 kids.

113   **Choose your own Christmas tree** to cut down while sipping cider in Apple Hill. Just to name a few: Harris Tree Farm, Hillside Tree Farm, or Santa's Acres.

114   Look at **rare books, photographs, maps** in the Rare Materials Reading Room and track your California genealogy at the California State Library, across of the Capitol. Bring a roll of quarters if you want to make copies of any microfilm.

115   Drop-in for an open play session at **Laguna's Awesome Party Place** in Elk Grove for inflatable castles, obstacle courses, slides, and arcade games. Must wear socks. $7 per child, Monday through Friday.

116   Memorize the differences between **Blue Oak, Live Oak, and Valley Oak** trees (*sactownkids. com/oaktrees*). See if you can spot them around Sacramento. We have oak trees everywhere!

117   Step back into the 1850s during the **Gold Rush Days** on Labor Day Weekend in September, when 28-acres of historic parkland in Old Sac turns into a time warp. People dressed in historic outfits and old-time music makes this a special day.

118   Make herbal tinctures, oils, and salves at an **Herbal Medicine Making** class. Ages 12 & up. *arconservancy.org*

119   Hike the easy, 2.2-mile **Salmon Falls Loop**, a fun
      nature walk through oak trees down to Folsom Lake.

120   **Toss a soft Beamo frisbee or play some lawn
      games** at a friendly local winery, like **Julietta Winery**
      in Clarksburg.

121   Take an **all-ages family hike** to the South Fork of the
      American River let by a naturalist with the American
      River Conservancy. The hike is 3 miles out and back,
      all-terrain strollers OK. $10 per family suggested
      donation.

122   Take a **free walking tour of Sandhill cranes**
      October through March at **Consumnes River
      Preserve**, provided by non-profit Save Our Sandhill
      Cranes and the Sacramento Audubon Society.

123   Find some plush fabric and a teddy bear pattern, and
      sew a few cuddly bears for some children in need.
      Drop them off at UC Davis Children's Hospital.

124   Go to the next **Free Girls Golf Clinic** at Haggin Oaks,
      Bing Maloney, or William Land golf courses.

125   Rent a **pontoon boat** at Rollins Lake in Colfax with
      another family for an afternoon of boating. An adult
      over 27 needs to have at least two years of boating
      experience to be able to rent a pontoon.

126   Go to a **"kids eat free"** night at a local restaurant, like Riverside Clubhouse in Land Park on Tuesdays. Plus Tuesday is taco night, what could be better.

127   **Get basic canoeing skills**, and find out what to do when you're in a capsized canoe, with a class at Sacramento State Aquatic Center. Ages 12 & up.

128   Go on a **full moon hike** with an REI guide. You'll take a nature adventure at a nearby park, guided by moonlight. Tours are 3 hours long. Ages 14 & up.

129   **Stay up late to watch the July 4th fireworks** at Cal Expo or Old Town Sacramento. The exciting explosions of color usually start at 9pm.

130   Enjoy the hands-on magic of woodworking at **The Woodshop** with real tools and real wood. Classes for kids ages 6 & up. *thewoodshop.us*

131   **Smell the Corpse Flower** plant when it blooms between May and August at the UC Davis Herbarium. It's the largest and stinkiest flower on the planet! Follow UCD Titan Arums on Facebook for bloom alerts.

132   Visit the **Blue Heron Trails,** Sacramento region's newest nature area near Elk Grove. A short, paved walkway is perfect for a morning walk away from the bustle of the city. The best time of year to view migratory birds is October through May.

133   Join the **Sacramento Tree Foundation** on a family-friendly Workday Event, where **kids can learn how to plant, weed, and mulch native plants**. Past events have included working on the Bear River Habitat Trail, where native plantings provide critical habitat for wildlife, and serves as beautiful foliage for a walking/biking path that connects neighborhoods around the City of Plumas Lake.

134   Swim or play "freeze tag" or "popsicle" in one of **Sacramento's 18 city park pools**. Admission is $2 for kids, $4 for adults, cash only.

135   **Celebrate Black History Month** in February with a great collection of free events by the Sacramento Public Library, showcasing illuminating interactive music, dance, and storytelling.

136   Treat comic book kid-fans to a morning at **Oblivion Comics & Coffee** on 11th St. It doesn't hurt that they carry **Chocolate Fish coffee** and deliver your latte with a Wonder Woman logo.

137   Drop by the **28th & B Skate Park** afterschool or on weekends for $3 per session of supervised **open skateboarding** on quarter pipes and rails. Or just watch some super-coordinated kids perform tricks. Helmets, elbow pads, and knee pads required; a limited quantity are available for rent for $1.

138   Visit the **"crown jewel"** of the Sacramento Public Library, the **Special Collections** in the 2nd Floor Sacramento Room at the Central Library on I Street. You can't borrow anything here, but you can carefully look at rare, historic books, photos, periodicals, postcards, and more. Ask a librarian for a few cool things to see.

139   Take a **Spooky Sacramento River Cruise** in your Halloween costume in October with Hornblower Cruises, and listen to creaky Halloween music while getting your face painted and taking in the sights and sounds of the river.

140   Watch a truly amazing ball game played by the elite San Francisco Giants **wheelchair softball** team, through the Paralympic Sport Sacramento Club. Prepare to be inspired.

141   **Make a flower press** with wood and screws and bolts and fill it with California poppies in the spring. *sactownkids.com/makeflowerpress*

142   What could be better than splashing, water gymnastics, and music? Watch the next show or competition by the **Sacramento Synchronized Swim Team**, and be wowed by their breathtaking athleticism and grace. If you want to try it out, join one of their beginner clinics. Ages 6 & up.

143   Get bitten by the acting bug with **New Star Children's Theatre**, which offers programs through the Fair Oaks, Folsom, and Sacramento Parks and Recreation departments. The junior program (ages 4-6) allows participants to have a small role in the current production, with no auditions required.

144   Go to family bounce night at **Bounce U** in Roseville or Rancho Cordova.

145   Get the chills looking up at the **110-foot high interior dome of the Cathedral of the Blessed Sacrament** on 11th & K St. Walk through the back hallways to see ancient scriptures in framed encasements on the wall. Tours to the public are given Wednesdays and Sundays, and include fascinating details of the building's history.

146   Visit the **Sacramento History Museum** and delve into the past 200 years of culture, technology, and everyday life in California with interactive exhibits. See how they used to print newspapers and mine for gold.

147   Watch **college students** tackle incredibly complex pieces of classical music at the UC Davis Symphony Orchestra. Concerts usually run monthly during the entire school year. $10 for 18 & under, $20 adults.

148   Get the knack of cool math shortcuts and tricks at **Mathnasium.**

149   Watch some **live rhythm & blues** with the kids in a
       rare non-bar setting at the awesome, kid-friendly **Out
       of the Box Festival** in the fall. Check the Sacramento
       Blues Society website for dates. *sacblues.com*

150   Become able to **play simple songs on the guitar**
       by taking guitar lessons at Kline Music or The Fifth
       String. Ages 6 & up.

151   Ever wonder how actors in musicals learn to sing and
       dance around the stage so effortlessly? Take a **Musical
       Theatre & Jazz** dance class at Capitol City Dance
       Academy, and find out what it takes! Ages 8 & up.

152   Bring some lawn games to the quaint **McConnell
       Estates Winery** in Elk Grove and relax next to the
       vineyard and their 100-year old red barn. Tasting
       room is open Fridays, Saturdays, and Sundays 11-
       5pm. Kids are also welcome to the annual chili cook-
       off and their annual concert series.

153   Visit your favorite museums in Sacramento on **free
       museum day**, usually in February. You can probably
       squeeze at least two in one day. Take a break for lunch
       and a long nap. *sactownkids.com/freemuseums*

154   **Learn how to ollie** at the next Sk8 Camp (ages
       5-18) at 28th & B St. Skate Park and meet other
       skaters from the region and acquire new tricks.
       Beginners and advanced skaters welcome. Register at
       cityofsacramento.org

155 Meet local artists and makers, and enjoy free music, at the **River City Marketplace** every year in April and October at various downtown parks.

156 Sniff **500 rare roses** at the Sacramento Historic Rose Garden in the **Old City Cemetery**, the oldest cemetery in Sacramento where many famous California pioneers are buried. Some of the antique roses were brought across the country on horse-drawn wagons. Free, docent-led cemetery history tours are held on some Saturdays. Maps and brochures for self-guided tours are available at the Archives Mortuary Chapel on the cemetery grounds. The Open Garden day kicks off rose season in April with free tours.

157 Go bird-watching along the **Grizzly Island Wildlife Area Trail**, a 4.5-mile easy and flat loop along the Sacramento Delta.

158   Drop in for some **Nepalese steamed dumplings and kulfi**, an ice cream made flavored with pistachio nuts and saffron, at Kathmandu Kitchen on Broadway.

159   Dig into July's pear season with a trip to a **u-pick pear orchard** in or around Courtland, like Double M Farms in Walnut Grove. $5 a bag, cash only, self-serve, no bathrooms.

160   Go to a free old-fashioned, family-friendly **country western dance party** in the streets of Old Sacramento in September, part of the Gold Rush Days celebration. Enjoy live music, and games like cornhole toss and giant jenga.

161   **Raise money for the Sacramento SPCA** in the annual 2K/5K Doggy Dash in Land Park in April. Food trucks, pet parades, and contests will get the kids laughing.

162   Elevate your **ping pong game** and bounce down to the **California Table Tennis Club** ($7 all day). Classes available for ages 6 & up, or you can watch the Rumble Tournament on the first Sunday of every month.

163   Be ready for some impressive (and sometimes slightly weird) Christmas lights display at the **Global Winter Wonderland** at Cal Expo. Be sure to catch the stage acrobatics shows – free with admission – to help justify the ticket prices.

164   Find out what's the best way to **spike a ball** with
the **Sacramento Youth Volleyball** program at
Reichmuth Park. Ages 7-15.

165   **Take a hayride at High Hill Ranch** in Apple Hill in
the fall and take a stroll through the craft fair open
seven days a week. Go on a weekday when the crowds
are thin and lines are short. Opens at the end of
August for pears and peaches. September and October
mainly feature apples. The pumpkin patch opens Oct.
1st.

166   Hike the 4-mile out-and-back **Avery's Pond Trail
for fantastic butterfly-viewing** and colorful
wildflowers in the spring. It's 20 miles from
Sacramento along the North Fork of the American
River, just above Folsom Lake.

167   Take older, art-inclined kids to the **Design Museum
at UC Davis** at Cruess Hall. New exhibits by faculty
and MFA grad students keep it fresh and fascinating.
Free. Check new events and exhibit info at:
arts.ucdavis.edu/design-museum

168   **Do one hour of clean-up** at your favorite
Sacramento park on **National Public Lands Day**
at the end of September, and help give back while
beautifying our region. About 30% of our country
is public land for all to enjoy. Find a family-friendly
organized clean-up like at Effie Yeaw Nature Center.

169   Every April, the **Sikh Parade** winds its way through Stockton, to end at the oldest Sikh temple in the United States. Colorful, elaborate floats, ethnic dances, and free Indian food make this event a must-see.

170   Get a whiff of delectable, mesmerizing exotic scents at **The Allspicery** spice house on 11th St. Grab their house-made hot cocoa mix to drink in front of the fireplace. Or get some cardamom pods, cinnamon sticks, and cloves for homemade chai on a chilly, winter day. Steep in warmed almond or cashew milk.

171   Book a free **45-minute session with a genealogist** (for free!) on Sundays at the Sacramento Public Library, and start uncovering interesting tidbits about your family's history.

172   Curl up with a blanket next to the pond for the free **Outdoor Movie Night at El Dorado Hills Town Center** in the summer.

173   Rent a bike at **City Bicycle Works** and explore Midtown. Get the Bikeway User Map at *cityofsacramento.org* for safe bike lanes.

174   Dig in to delicious noodle and rice dishes at the **Filipino Fiesta** in June.

175   Explore advanced scientific concepts using a variety of tools with the **Science Club** at the Sacramento Public Library. This event occurs once a month, check the Events calendar at *saclibrary.org*. Past lessons and activities include paleontology and a fossil making workshop. All materials are provided. Ages 8-12.

176   Have a **snowball fight after a fresh snowfall** in the winter at nearby Echo Lake.

177   Join the **Summer Reading program** at the Sacramento Public Library, log all the books you read, and win prizes every step of the way.

178   See a play, musical, or dance at your **local high school's theatre program**. You'll be amazed at all the high school talent we have in Sacramento.

179   Take diving lessons and **work up to doing a fun back dive with half twist**. Local USA Diving Clubs include Capital Divers and Dos Rios Divers. Dede Crayne of Capital Divers tells us that within a few lessons most kids will jump forward and backward off the 1-meter and 3-meter boards. From there they will learn to do inward dives, reverse dives, front and back flips, and twisting. Generally, they are amazed at all that is learned fairly quickly. They also use a trampoline and do some conditioning. Discover the fun of diving!

180   Visit **Kid's Town at Mill View Ranch** in Apple Hill, where you can explore a countryside mini-city, built just for little humans.

181   Celebrate the Emancipation Proclamation's historical liberation of slaves and the ongoing legacy of freedom and community among all Americans at the **Sacramento Juneteenth Festival** in June. Through artwork, performances, and hands-on activities, kids learn about this important point in our nation's history.

182   Support local theatre and visit **Runaway Stage Production's** new Children's Storybook Theatre in West Sacramento, or participate in their Youth Musical Theatre Workshop.

183   Visit and urban community garden plot, like **Bean Jr. Memorial Park** on 17th Ave. You'll find dwarf fruit trees, herbs, and vegetables to touch and smell. Keep your eyes open for butterflies and earth-friendly critters.

184   Watch **Sacramento's largest firework display** at Old Sac's Waterfront at 9pm on New Year's Eve. Go earlier for food, face-painting, live music, and exciting street entertainment, especially if the kids won't make it past 9:30pm!

185   Take your dog on a 2-mile walk along the American River Parkway at the **Howlin' on the Parkway** event in April, complete with pet vendors, food trucks, and – of course – the pet costume contest. The costumes are never as amazing as the fact that the dogs agree to wear them.

186   Dress up like a character out of Oliver Twist, and step back in time for the annual **Victorian Christmas in Nevada City**. Stop by the Crystal Rainbow Rock Shop, hidden in ivy like a secret treasure cave.

187   **Rent a GoPro** camera at the Arcade Public Library's "Library of Things", and record your day's adventure of running, jumping, riding, sliding, and anything else you can imagine. Edit your video to music and show your grandparents.

188   Meet award-winning ceramicists, glass, and metal artists in person at the **Art by Fire "Seconds Sale"** the second Saturday in January, where they sell their less-than-perfect mugs, pots, and artwork at the Shepard Garden and Art Center. Teach kids that **mistakes can be beautiful.**

189   Dress up in some vintage frocks and take some wacky family photos at **O'Grady's Old Time Photos** or **McGee's Old Time Photos** in Old Sacramento. Buy some postcards while you're being a tourist, and send them to far-away relatives.

190   Buzz over to the **California Honey Festival** in
      Woodland for bee-friendly gardening tips, a busy
      bee kids stage, honey tastings, food, wine, and beer.
      Usually held in April or May.

191   Have a wood-burning oven pizza lunch in the
      vineyard just 15 miles away at Scribner's Bend
      Winery's **"Weekends at the Vineyard,"** Saturdays
      and Sundays 11-4pm. Check current schedule for
      live music performers. Or just go with a picnic
      basket anytime for lush scenery of their vineyard
      and landscaped gardens. Their tasting room is open
      Friday through Sunday. Dogs welcome.

192   Pick up the endlessly fascinating book, **The Outdoor
      World of the Sacramento Region**, a full-color
      illustrated guide to Sacramento area wildlife. Trust
      me, a gem. Every time you see a bird, duck, insect, or
      wildflower, you can try to identify it and read about
      some interesting facts. It even has pictures of the
      different scat droppings you might find on nature
      trails. If you don't know what scat is, you need this
      book. Published by the American River Natural
      History Association.

193   Watch **board-breaking and sparring** at the annual
      Robinson's Tae Kwon Do Championships, usually in
      February, open to the public.

194   **Look for caterpillars** at Sutter's Landing River Access Park.

195   Throw a **frisbee** at any wide open park, like East Portal Park or Land Park. Keep a foldable frisbee with you at all times for anytime/anywhere fun.

196   Rent a kayak and **paddle down the Sacramento River** from Broderick Boat Ramp to the Sacramento Marina. 2 hours, tandem for two, $75, includes kayak drop-off and pick-up. *kayaking.fit*

197   Go shopping for art supplies and buy extras to take to the **Mustard Seed School**, a free private school for homeless children ages 3-15. Check their current needs at *sacloaves.org*

198   See the world through amber-colored glasses at the **Auburn Mandarin Festival** in November. Some of the best and sweetest mandarins in the world come from the hills of Placer County. From the mandarin scones to the mandarin pizza, mandarin BBQ sauce, mandarin salad dressings – you will leave inspired by the versatility of this mild citrus fruit. They say that Placer's popular Owari Satsuma mandarins contain synephrine, a natural antihistamine that relieves cold and allergy symptoms.

199   Go on a fall bird walk at **Knickerbocker Creek** with the ARC Conservancy, and see songbirds, raptors, and water birds. Free with suggested donation. Ages 8 & up.

200   Bundle up in fall and winter for a traditional tea gathering at the **Sokiku Nakatani Tea Room & Garden** at California State University, Sacramento. Take in Japanese aesthetics and traditional arts, and Chado, the way of tea. Ages 8 & up.

201   Hike towards **Galena Falls** for a dazzling display of wildflowers in the first mile in the summertime. The actual waterfall is another 1.5 miles away, which makes this hike more suitable for older kids, 6 & up.

202   Visit **Dilly Dally** the effervescent clown who creates unique and super-cute balloon animals at Davis Farmer's Market every Saturday morning at Central Park in Davis. *dillydallytheclown.com*

203   See the free, outdoor narrated performance of **T'was the Night Before Christmas** on balconies and rooftops in Old Sac at Historic Sacramento's Theatre of Lights. Check dates in December.

204   **Light a lantern and take a walk** around your block just as the sun sets over Sacramento and listen to little nighttime sounds. Listen for the **American Crow bird**, which gathers into roosts (sleeping groups) at night. They are one of the most intelligent bird species and very common in Sacramento neighborhoods. If you're brave enough to go at night (in a safe neighborhood, or just your front yard) then **look for glistening worms** weaving in and out of the dirt, having an all-night party.

205   **Race boats down the stream** at Dry Creek, which runs alongside Gibson Ranch County Park. Test your boat-building skills using recycled materials you find around the house, like paper plates, paper cups, plastic containers, and cardboard. Find inspiration and tips online.

206   **Road-trip to Napa and stay in a yurt at Bothe-Napa Valley State Park** and take a dip in the spring-fed swimming pool. Hike easy trails among redwoods, oak trees, maples, and madrones. The Native American Plant Garden is a short, easy trail for kids. $60-75 per night.

207   Swing on ropes and stand in the mist of a small waterfall at the kid-friendly **Happy Valley swimming hole** along the Consumnes River.

208   Get an outdoor day pass to **California Family Fitness** in Elk Grove and swim to your heart's content in three pools (including one outdoor heated pool open in the winter) and a jacuzzi. Play some beach volleyball on a sand court, basketball, and tennis. $8 per person for pool access, or sign-up for a free trial week.

209   Get the giggles out with a laugh-out-loud play or musical at the kid-friendly **24th Street Theatre**.

210   Adventure your way to **becoming an Eagle Scout**.

211   See the majestic Sierra Nevada Foothills from a **hot air balloon** with Sky Drifters in Rancho Murieta.

212   Road trip to Galt in May for the **Strawberry Festival** and take part in an early pancake breakfast, carnival games, live music, chef demonstrations, car show, kids zone, and a Miss. & Mr. Strawberry Pageant. Past festivals have also included Frisbee Dogs (yes, dogs playing frisbees) and an Aerial Assault Trampoline Exhibition.

213   Take some **gourmet pizza** to go at Hot Italian, OneSpeed, Hot City Pizza, Obo, Pieology, ZPizza, or your favorite Sacramento pizzaria.

214   Make some homemade popcorn, grab a picnic blanket, and go to a free summer movie at **Friday Flicks at Roseville's Vernon Street Town Square**.

215   Teach kids the importance of staying on the trail when hiking in Sacramento, and looking out for snakes. Learn the important steps to take if someone gets a **rattlesnake bite**, it could save your life. *https://www.wikihow.com/Treat-a-Rattlesnake-Bite*

216   Life with kids is a "comedy of errors." In July, take your accidental comedians down to the **Sacramento Shakespeare Festival** with a blanket and picnic and enjoy the magical splendor of outdoor theater at the William A. Carroll Amphitheater in Land Park. Kids 6-12 free. Only kids 6 & above are allowed. They are strict about this age minimum.

217   **"Brunch with the Birds"** at Blue Heron Trails, part of the Stone Lakes National Wildlife Refuge. Friends of Stone Lakes periodically host a free open house for 2 hours, where you can take a docent-let nature walk and learn about all the rare species flourishing along this area of the Pacific Flyway. There's something happening during every season. Winter is the best time to see migratory wildlife, like geese, cranes, sandpipers, and plovers.

218   Camp all year-round at **Orchard Springs Campground on Rollins Lake**, complete with showers, a clubhouse, boat rentals, and an event stage. Volleyballs are free to use. Bundle up in blankets at the Meadow for the family-friendly Saturday Movie Night.

219   Walk, run, or in-line skate across Folsom's beautiful historic **Truss Bridge**. Make your way to the ever-popular, iconic **Karen's Bakery** before jetting home.

220   Go to the **Sac Anime Comic-Con** costume contest in January and marvel at the meticulous creativity of local comic fans. Or just people watch in the lobby and roam the halls of the convention center, where there is plenty at which to gawk.

221   **Immerse in the French language through role-play**, games, songs, and crafts in children's classes at the magical French school, Alliance Française de Sacramento.

222   Get or borrow some pop-up soccer goals, get some friends together and **play 3-on-3 soccer** at a peaceful, riverside park like Larchmont Community Park.

223   Enter a family **Halloween costume contest** in October, like the annual Auburn Community Festival.

224 Run around 100 picturesque acres of lush greenery and wildlife at the **UC Davis Arboretum**. The East Asian, Australian, and Middle East Collections are especially beautiful. The 3.5-mile loop trail is easy and flat. Download the map of gardens online before going.

225 Kick it with the **Sacramento Republic FC** soccer team players and coaches at their next kids clinic or camp. Events for kids are usually in the summer. Check their online Upcoming Events calendar. Ages 6 & up.

226 Make a splash at the **baby-friendly wading pools** at Sacramento city parks. Your baby will have a ball and sleep better, and you won't be quite as stressed-out (fingers-crossed!). *sactownkids.com/wading pools*

227 Skate your winter blues away at **Winter Wonderland Ice Skating Event** at Skatetown Ice Arena in Roseville. Past events have included games, prices, holiday music with a live DJ, laser light show, black lights, and a great big pile of snow.

228 **Attend a star party**, eclipse viewing, meteor shower viewing, or new moon celebration with the **Sacramento Valley Astronomical Society**. They usually host a Star-B-Q in July!

229   **Dress up like a wild animal** and run through Land Park in the Sacramento Zoo Zoom 5k/10k Kids' Fun Run in March, and get free admission to the zoo at the end.

230   Get a fascinating peek at artists' studios at an open studios event, like **Sac Open Studios** in the summertime or the **Amador County Open Studios Tour**.

231   Visit the **Wakamatsu Tea and Silk Farm Colony** in Placerville, the first Japanese colony in the U.S. originating in 1869. The 272-acre property features an 1850s farmhouse and barn. The rolling oak woodlands and lake with a 1.5-mile wheelchair and stroller accessible trail is a perfect weekend escape. Find their next Wakamatsu Open Farm Day. $10 per vehicle. *arconservancy.org*.

232   Cut **u-pick sunflowers** in the summertime at Goyette's North Canyon Ranch.

233   Take the city's light rail to the most-frequented stop in downtown – the **Ice Blocks Midtown** on the R Street Corridor. Grab a beignet from Milk Money, a coffee from Philz, and watch the light rail trains go by.

234   Grab your wickets and stakes for a game of **croquet** at any Sacramento city park. Invite multiple families for a truly worthwhile, chaotic croquet experience.

235 Chow down at the **Sacramento Nachos Festival** in August and taste over 40 different nachos recipes, jive to some live music, and check out the game area for kids.

236 **Rent the Baby Lock sewing machine** at the Arcade Public Library's "Library of Things" and sew a super-simple baby blanket, tea towel, or try a more ambitious family project.

237 Bounce your way through obstacle courses at Friday family fun night at the **Bounce Spot** in West Sacramento.

238 Go on a guided pony ride at **Penryn Oak Stables**, a beautiful 25-acre working horse ranch, about 30 minutes northeast of Sacramento.

239 Want to **see a drone up close**? Join the Sacramento Drone Access on MeetUp.com and meet local drone enthusiasts who are willing to share their knowledge and do a demonstration for you.

240 **See the earliest telephones** at the Roseville Telephone Museum, one of the largest collections of antique telephones in the nation, including wooden box, coffin, magneto, and three-box telephones. Don't miss the cool switchboard exhibit.

241   Go on a **Bird Walk for Novices** with the Yolo Audubon Society. Ages 5 & up.

242   Teens and older can peruse healing crystals and stones and **get a tarot card reading** at the annual Healing Expo or Holistic Holiday Market.

243   Make anything your imagination can dream up at **ReCreate's Open Art Studio**, where kids can use **unlimited recycled art materials** for $6.75/hour. Examples of fairy houses and rocket ships are on display to spark the imagination. ReCreate uses technology and sustainability principles to teach the next generation of makers, scientists, and artists, while also diverting more than 60 tons of materials that local businesses would have otherwise tossed into landfills.

244   Find a kid-friendly fun run or charity race, like the **Pear Fair Fun Run** (1/2 mile for kids) the last Sunday in July.

245   String bike lights on your bikes and go for a **moonlit ride with Lunar Lunacy** along iconic Sacramento landmarks in August.

246   Take a **90-minute real train ride** on Amtrak to San Francisco (Emeryville) for about $30.

247   Wear a fancy hat and **have a tea party with friends** at a tea room like Dash of Panache or Tea Xotics.

248   Head out to Camino Ridge (Snows Road at Fuji Court) in Apple Hill for **u-pick blueberries** on weekends the last week of June through mid-July.

249   Experience life as a kid in the 1800s and visit the **Old Sacramento Schoolhouse Museum** and see relics of a centuries-old classroom.

250   Take the next free **farm tour at Farm Fresh To You** in Capay Valley, just 45 minutes away, and see with your own eyes how our food is grown. Harvest activities, tractor rides, and gorgeous scenery.

251   Go **wildflower hunting at Frog Lake** on the south side of Carson Pass near Lake Tahoe. Hike in about one mile from the parking area.

252   Uncover some long-lost, 100-year old vintage treasures at the **Sacramento Antique Faire**. See what an old-fashioned iron and laundry machine looked like. *Hint: It's not a machine.*

253   Walk across (or just look at) **Foresthill Bridge, the tallest bridge in California**, that towers over the North Fork American River. Grab a delicious piece of country pie at Ikeda's or grandma's bread pudding at Awful Annie's in Auburn.

254   Go to the **Eggstravaganza Easter Egg Hunt** with multiple hunts and a myriad of activities for kids in April at Fairytale Town.

255   Collect all the socks you don't use anymore and take it to **Sac Sock Drop's** charity drive to help those in need of socks during the winter season. The drive usually takes place in early-to-mid December. Check *uptownstudios.net* for drop-off location.

256   Drive out to **Soil Born Farms** at American River Ranch in Rancho Cordova for their annual **Day at the Farm** event with tours, workshops, cooking classes, and kids gardening activities, and a plant sale. Bring your bikes, scooters, or in-line skates and access the American River bike path next to Hagan Park, across the street. Admission $5.

257   Download the latest Solano BikeLinks Map from the Solano Transit Authority and find **off-street bike paths** and recommended routes for children and families in Davis, like the Fairfield Linear Park bike path, and ride away!

258   See high-speed, **supersonic aircraft performances** at the California Capital Airshow at Mather Field in September. Modern fighter jets and vintage warbirds go head to head.

259   Spread delight. **Leave a colorful drawing** or uplifting message of love on a park bench at your favorite Sacramento park. Someone who needs it will take it home.

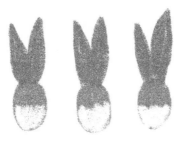

260   Take in some beautiful sounds at a **Northern California Children's Chorus** concert. Past concerts have included interesting instruments you don't see too often, like organ, harp, Irish fiddle, strings, and African drums. Some concerts are free for children under 12.

261   Paint blank ceramic pieces at **Alpha Fired Arts**. Get inspired by art that you like, or write a few lines from your favorite poem. Personalize it for someone you love. Wanna live it up with a little gold? After having your piece fired (it takes up to two weeks), paint some gold flecks or decorations on it by buying some Duncan OG 801 Bright Gold Overglaze (2 grams for $30) and painting some gold on your piece. Ask them to fire it again at a very low temperature. It's a spendy project, so you may want to do this with some friends and split the cost.

262   Celebrate **Taco Tuesday** at your favorite Mexican spot, like La Venadita, Chando's Tacos, Taqueria Espinoza, Zocalo, Tres Hermanas… or try a new establishment in your neck of the woods.

263   Join the **Great Grape Crush** at the Lodi Grape Festival in September. 5 & under free.

264   Develop resilience, mentorships, and healthy habits in small groups with **SMART Girls** at the Boys and Girls Club Sacramento. Ages 8-18.

265   Go to **Bannister Park** in Fair Oaks and walk/bike/scooter down the beautiful 1-mile paved trail to the picnic tables along the American River, where ducks, birds, fish, and big climbing rocks await.

266   Read topographic lines and **find out how to use a map without a compass** at REI's Backcountry Navigation classes at Deer Creek Hills Nature Preserve. 9am-3pm. Teens allowed with a parent.

267   Browse a locally owned art store like **University Art**, and get ideas for your next family art project.

268   Sit on pillows and low tables and eat with your hands at the Kasbah Lounge on J St. Have a **Middle Eastern feast** of falafels, hummus, baba ghanoush, warm flat bread, and baklava desserts. Kids will love the bananas beignets too, little banana doughnuts with a scoop of ice cream and butterscotch sauce.

269   Older teens interested in archaeology can **go on a local archaeology tour** or talk hosted by the Sacramento Archaeological Society, with a parent or an adult. Past events have included a Vasco Caves Rock Art Tour (65 miles away), led by Naturalist Eddie Williams.

270   Buy some extra toothpaste, shampoo, and bar soap for homeless people and families in need, and drop them off at **Loaves and Fishes**, 1351 North C Street, Monday through Friday, 7am-3pm.

271   Get a **classic children's novel** like by C.S. Lewis, Roald Dahl, or J.K. Rowling at a cozy used bookstore like **Beers Books**. Start reading it in the stacks. Take it home and get lost in an imaginary world of wizardry and magic.

272   **Shadow a prosecutor**, investigator, or judge in the **Sacramento's District Attorney's office**. The DA has created a youth program, Criminal Justice Shadow Day, where Sacramento County high school students are paired with a worker in the justice system to learn the job role, depending on the student's area of interest. There is also a presentation on crime scene investigations, evidence collection, and forensic science. Find out when their next program starts and register early to apply. *sacda.org*

273   **Rent some bikes in Old Sac at Practical Bikes** and explore the waterfront, downtown, and beyond.

274   Get some metallic origami paper from Oto's Japanese grocer on Freeport Blvd. and **learn how to make a gold crane**, a symbol of good luck.

275   Get a good grip and cruise down some snow on a **toboggan** at **Adventure Mountain**, at the top of Echo Summit off of Highway 50. Where can you find a toboggan? Home Depot usually has them in the playsets & recreation department.

276   Take a kids **judo class** at Capital City Judo. Ages 3 & up.

277   Take the elevator to the 15th floor at the Hyatt in downtown Sacramento to **see the city view from the Capitol View Room**. It's open if there are no events, but call ahead to verify.

278   Take a **family handstand lesson** with Handstand Nation in East Sacramento, and learn fun tricks about balance. Do partner work, inversions, and flying yoga. Starting at $15/per family member. *thehandstandnation.com*

279   **Whack a bucket of practice balls** at the beautifully serene Ancil Hoffman Golf Course.

280   Take one of seemingly **endless nature walks** at the
       upper and lower Sunrise Recreation Areas near Fair
       Oaks. Take a walk or bike ride across the red, historic
       Fair Oaks Bridge.

281   See a family-friendly flick at a **historic, old-
       fashioned movie theater** like Tower Theatre.
       Enjoy an enchanting pre-show dinner or lunch at the
       worldly **Tower Cafe**. Ask to sit it on the upper patio
       under tree branches and string lights. Bring pennies
       for the kids to toss into the fountain.

282   Get a **tie-dye kit** at Dick Blick Art Materials on Fulton
       Ave. and spend the afternoon getting your dye on.

283   Celebrate the **Chinese New Year** in February and
       watch a dragon dance, ethnic dance, martial arts, and
       choral music at the Sacramento Chinese New Year
       Celebration, the largest Chinese community event in
       Northern California.

284   **Play chess** on the Avid Reader at Broadway Station
       bookstore's chess table. Find at a book on how to play
       chess.

285   Get ready for **preschool at the Zoo**. Go to a Little
       Peeps class (ages 3-5) at the Sacramento Zoo,
       and learn about animal habitats through stories,
       song, and crafts. A special visit from an "animal
       ambassador" is usually the highlight.

286   Catch a bus or train down to Old Sac for the famous family-friendly **Sacramento Music Festival** for Memorial Day at the end of May, and see over 100 unique performances from all kinds of different genres from jazz to rock to bluegrass, plus animated parades, street dancing, and food.

287   Go down to the annual **Sacramento Chocolate Salon** in January, and feast your eyes on imaginative chocolate creations by artisans near and far. Meet chocolatiers and stay for a free demo. Kids under 6 are free (2 kids per adult).

288   Get a **haircut on a mini-motorcycle** or open-top jeep car at the Jack n Jillybeans Salon in Rocklin or Roseville.

289   **Start a family piggy bank** and save up for something special, like a trip to Lake Tahoe or tickets to a show at the new Golden 1 Arena. Teach kids the power of compound interest.

290   **Rent a batting cage** to practice your pitches and home runs at East Field in El Dorado Hills. Bring your own helmet, bat, and balls. $15 for one hour. *eldoradohillscsd.org*

291   See a **blacksmith demonstration** and pan for gold at Pioneer Village, an outdoor interpretive center at the Folsom History Museum.

292   Get the early crop of **u-pick apples** mid-September at Apple Hill. Find a u-pick farm, like Goyette's North Canyon Ranch, where you can pluck apples right off the trees. Go to *applehill.com* for current u-pick listings.

293   Watch a family-favorite musical like Beauty and the Beast, on stage at **Davis Musical Theatre Company**.

294   Get free admission to the **Skate Park in Community Park** in El Dorado Hills, where novice and advanced skaters are welcome. Must register with a signed waiver. Pads and helmets available to borrow. Hours vary, check before going.

295   Rent a professional-grade camera and nice lens (like the 50mm f2.8) from **Mike's Camera**, borrow a tripod, and take as many family portraits and candid shots as you can over a weekend. Ask them to show you how to use the self-timer and continuous mode to shoot ten pictures at a time, and capture that perfect shot.

296   Explore more than 4,000 acres of grasslands, oak woodlands, and seasonal creeks at **Deer Creek Park**.

297   **Go ghost-hunting.** Visit the 2nd floor of the California State Library. Legend has it that the California section is haunted by an older gentleman ghost with glasses, poring over books.

298   Go on a **full moon kayak paddle** at sunset on Lake Natoma with Current Adventures.

299   Explore the riparian (riverside) habitats at **William B. Pond Recreation Area**. Fish for trout, catfish, bass, bluegill, and tule perch in the man-made pond.

300   Ride the **Polar Express** in December, six train cars pulled by vintage diesels from the **California State Railroad Museum's** collection. The El Dorado Observation Car might be the best for little wiggly ones, as it's divided into two sections: The Parlor and Lounge. You can move around and step off onto the observation deck at the "North Pole" at the end of the train ride.

301   Visit the children's section and read some inspiring books at **Underground Books** on 35th St. in Oak Park. Then share a lavender lemonade next door at **Old Soul** and run around at **McClatchy Park**, which has an awesome 9-hole disc golf course, by the way.

302   Slither around with more than 45 venomous reptiles including **Black Mamba and King Cobra snakes** at the annual Sacramento Reptile Show in the fall. Their reptile education center teaches you about all the different species.

303   **Dance on the lawn at Bogle Vineyards** during their summer Al Fresco Friday events. Wine tastings, live music, food trucks, and kids running alongside rows of grapes. A perfect setting to snap some memorable sunset pictures. $15 adults, $5 kids.

304   Take a **self-transformation art workshop at The Creation District**, a community-focused art school created by Walking the Village, the nonprofit that also runs the Tubman House, a home for young homeless parents. For teens.

305   **Train in basic bike repair** at the Sacramento Bicycle Kitchen's free classes. You'll be able to fix a flat, adjust your brakes, and do basic maintenance on the fly. Teens only, with a parent. They also have a free, all-ages second Saturday concert series in the summer.

306   Warm up on a rainy day with **Vietnamese pho noodle soup** at a Vietnamese eatery like Pho Bac Hoa Viet, Pho Saigon, Coriander Grill, or Star Ginger.

307   Go **snowshoeing** with easy rentals and lessons at Northstar-at-Tahoe, Sierra-at-Tahoe, and Royal George.

308   **Catch a glimpse of Victorian life** and tour the opulent Leland Stanford Mansion. It used to be the governor's official office before the State Capitol was built.

309   Rent the Ultimate Diazo Fabric **Screen Printing Kit** from the Sacramento Public Library's "Library of Things" and turn a line drawing, favorite quote, or bold intersection of shapes into a modern t-shirt.

310   Go to a real, traveling **Broadway show** at the Sacramento Convention Center.

311   Eat some baklava (pastries) and dolmathes (grape leaf rolls) and **dance under the stars at the Greek Festival of Sacramento** block party at the Greek Orthodox Church of the Annunciation in October. The event is modeled after a *panigiri*, a vibrant outdoor celebration of life with music and dancing that usually takes place in the center of Greek villages.

312   **Rent a Fender FA-100 Acoustic Guitar** from Sacramento Public Library's "Library of Things" and memorize the G, D, Em, and C chords. Otherwise known as I-V-vi-IV, a popular chord progression used in many pop songs.

313 Celebrate food and culture from the Mediterranean at the annual **Mediterranean Food Festival** in Rancho Cordova at the St. Stephen Orthodox Church. $3, Free for kids 10 & under. *ststephensofsac.com*

314 **Enter a doll's world** at one of the only dollhouse shops in the area. The **Elegant Dollhouse** on Fulton Ave. is were you'll find everything miniature. They also carry a full line of dollhouse kits, dollhouse lumber, dollhouse lighting, and how-to-miniature books. They've been open for 30+ years and are one of the best dollhouse stores in the California.

315 Practice all your newly acquired, bizarre dance moves at **Sing Along with Mister Cooper** at various public library locations. His newest album "The Color of Us" is available at *mistercooper.com* and Pandora.

316 Rent a **Toca 10" hand drum** from Sacramento Public Library's "Library of Things" and experiment with a few basic drum patterns. Watch some YouTube videos on basic drumming.

317 Meet some friends and slide into a pool of plastic balls at **Wacky Tacky** in Rancho Cordova or Roseville.

318 **Inspire a budding sewist** at the annual **Quilt, Craft & Sewing Festival** in March. Intricate, artistic designs bursting with color and geometry will give you quilt ideas to last a lifetime. $10 for 3 days.

319   **Get Apple Hill-savvy.** Go to *applehill.com* and
download the app to your device for up-to-the-minute
weather, traffic, and farm hours.

320   **Play disc golf (9-holes)** at Regency Community Park
in Natomas.

321   **See a play atop a mountain!** Every late spring
through early summer, a musical is staged at the top
of Mt. Tamalpais, with the San Francisco bay and
heavenly clouds in the background, by **Mountain
Play at the Cushing Memorial Amphitheater**. Buy
tickets in advance, bring a picnic, and get there early.
Past productions include Peter Pan, Sound of Music,
and Wizard of Oz, and Beauty and the Beast. It takes
early planning and a couple hours of driving, but it's
definitely a memory-maker.

322   **Discover how water travels** from your bathroom to
the rivers, creeks, and waterways around Sacramento
at the **Roseville Utility Exploration Center**. Check
out the game room and play Pollinator Relay, Creek
Patrol and Leap Frog.

323   See and touch a wide variety of **gems and unpolished
rocks** at the annual Roseville Gem, Jewelry, Fossil,
and Mineral Show in March by the Roseville Rock
Rollers Gem & Mineral Society. Check out the
exhibits, demonstrations, and kids' activities. Free
for kids 12 & under.

324   Get messy at **The Art Box** in Fair Oaks, a creative
        studio for kids with different themes each month, like
        Paint with the Dinosaurs, Gardening, Construction,
        & Under The Sea.

325   Watch your doggie play water sports with other dogs
        at the **Doggie Dip Day at Sacramento City Pools**.
        Doggie treats, pet contests, and doggie lifeguards are
        on-hand for the festivities. Check the current catalog
        for the next event.

326   Take extra craft supplies and new toys that you
        won't be using to **Women's Empowerment**, an
        organization that helps homeless women and their
        children get back on their feet.
        womensempowerment.org

327   **Is your stuffed animal ready for their own
        sleepover?** Prep your little stuffed friend for the next
        sleepover event at the public library in Carmichael.
        Soothe their fears and kiss them goodnight, then
        come back to pick them up in the morning, where
        they will be waiting, safe and sound.

328   Become a **foster family for a pet** in need. If your
        household can't manage a pet full-time but the kids
        are begging for a cat or dog, provide a temporary
        home for a homeless cat or dog for 3 weeks. Contact
        Sacramento Front Street Animal Shelter or sign-
        up online at *sacpetsearch.com*

329 In January or Feburary, wander around the **Home & Landscape Expo for family-friendly gardening ideas**, and let the kids do some interactive activities in the Karden Garden kids center. Learn how to build a sensory garden for kids and choose plants that inspire the imagination. Check schedule for details. Sometimes you can get free tickets in advance through the Sacramento Tree Foundation.

330 **Go on a casting audition** for a local theatre company, like **Roseville's Stand Out Talent** at the Roseville Historic Tower Theatre.

331 Drop-in to **Michaels** craft store's **Kids Club Saturdays** 10am-12pm for a new, seasonal craft every week. They craft while you shop. $2, supplies included, ages 3 & up. You can pre-register online.

332 In the fall and spring, **spot the migrating birds** using Mather Field lakes and ponds as a rest stop. Don't forget your binoculars.

333 Young, budding guitarists can see professional **guitar trios and ensembles** play in an up-close setting with no distractions at the intimate, live shows at The Fifth String Music Store on N Street. $12 tickets, recommended for teens & up.

334   Experience the heart-thumping drama of **dragon dances and taiko drumming** at the **Locke Asian Pacific Spring Festival** in the rural Chinese-built town of Locke, listed in the National Register of Historic Places. Free.

335   Visit the quaint but fascinating **Folsom State Prison Museum** for $2, which Johnny Cash penned a song about in "Folsom Prison Blues." Read inmates' letters and show the kids what a real prison cell looks like. Marvel at inmate's artistic creations, including a bouquet of roses made out of toilet paper, and a giant ferris wheel made out of toothpicks. Kids free, cameras welcome.

336   Have a **party in the car at a car wash** on a conveyor belt with colorful lights at a Quick Quack Car Wash. Bring a few Q-tips to keep the kids busy with interior detailing while you vacuum out the inside.

337   **Play pickleball** at R. Burnett Miller Park in East Sacramento. Bring your own paddles and balls. Tennis racquets work in a pinch.

338   Every last Saturday of the month, the Sacramento Zoo hosts a **Nature Explorers** program between 10am - 2pm, with changing themes, an open play area, storytime, crafts and activities. Free with admission.

339   Play **bocce ball** at the East Portal Bocce Club. A $40 membership gets you access for a year, plus you can bring in two guests at a time. Kids under 18 must be accompanied by an adult.

340   **Help wrap holiday gifts for families in need** at the Boys & Girls Club Santa Land Gift Wrapping Party in December, a perfect family service project. Complimentary holiday cookies, music, hot cocoa, and cider served. *bgcsac.org*

341   **Get your fishtails out for the annual Sacramento Promenade of Mermaids** at Old Sacramento Riverfront Park in May for a sea parade of mermaids, mermen, face painting, crafts, photo booths, and games. The costumes alone are quite a spectacular sight.

342   Hear **four-part harmonies and barbershop music** sung by about a hundred women in bold, colorful costumes with the Sacramento Valley Chorus. They also have rehearsals open to the public, weekly Wednesdays 6:30-9:30pm at the DDSO Hall in Arden-Arcade at 2231 St. Mark's Way.

343   Get some herbs to grow in the spring at the ever-cool **Plant Foundry in Oak Park**, or grow some lemons, limes, blood oranges, and Satsuma mandarins during the cold season.

344 Sign up for the next **Deer & Fawn storytime** at Effie Yeaw Nature Center. Kids ages 3 and 4 will love exploring the nature center, making crafts, singing songs, and possibly meeting a real, rehabilitated animal.

345 Get lost in the rows of gently used books at **Dimple Books** on Arden Way, and pick up a biography of someone with an interesting life.

346 Go snow tubing down **Blizzard Mountain** in a giant donut at Sierra-at-Tahoe. Kids under 42" free.

347 **Plant a tree.** Sacramento residents are eligible to receive up to 10 free shade trees, providing community and shade and reducing energy needs. *sactree.com*

348 Got your own bow? **Practice your archery skills** at the spacious archery range at Discovery Park.

349 For a short, 15-minnute hike with some of the best Lake Tahoe views, try **Cave Rock** on the southeastern shore. You can skip the scramble to the top, if you have small children. It's a sacred spot to the Washoe Indians, who call it the "Lady of the Lake" because from a distance, the rock looks like a woman's profile.

350 Throw down some new **Hip Hop** moves at Step 1 Dance & Fitness in downtown Sacramento. Ages 7-17.

351   Play a **family game of soccer**, or get some friends together to just run around a big, open field, like Granite Regional Park.

352   Brings scooters, bikes, and a harmonica down to **Discovery Park** and free-wheel down the **Jedediah Smith Bike Trail**, or at least a very small strip of it. Blow dandelions, make a wish, and look for ladybugs, praying mantis, and dragonflies. View a detailed map at *arpf.org*

353   Take a **family raft ride** down 7 stories, with 3 giant drops, at the Thunder Falls at Golfland SunSplash. Must be 48".

354   Chomp on some sweet treats at the **Sacramento Donut Festival** in September.

355   Get out with the baby and see some beauty at the **Baby Loves Art** class at the Crocker Art Museum.

356   Walk, blade, or bike across the Guy A. West Memorial Bridge, the **longest pedestrian suspension bridge in the U.S.** It's structurally similar to the Golden Gate Bridge in San Francisco, but you can have a mini-picnic in the middle and enjoy the river rushing below, without thousands of cars rushing by.

357   Head over to Roseville's Top Golf for some **over-the-top golf fun**. The only other Top Golf is in Las Vegas.

358   Get essential tips on how to **survive a zombie apocalypse**. Master disaster preparedness and valuable survival techniques at this 90-minute free class at REI, sometimes offered on Halloween. Recommended for teens with a parent.

359   On a cold winter day, warm up with some **steamy ramen noodles** at Shoki Ramen House, Ryujin Ramen House, or your favorite ramen eatery.

360   Rent the **Behringer DeepMind 12 Synthesizer** from Sacramento Public Library's "Library of Things" and make new sounds by piecing together the crunch of potato chips and rain boots splashing in water.

361   Join the **Kids Club at Arden Fair Mall** and join in on free monthly activity and shows. Register at Guest Services in front of JCPenney. Or go on a rainy day and ride the carousel and then check out the indoor kids' playground at the food court.

362   Check for the next **children's author reading** and signing at **Time Tested Books** on 21st St. Or just visit the Science section and find something cool to discover, like clouds, spiders, or Jupiter. Take a peek at their rare collection, and experience what old books smell like. Treat them like the treasures they are.

363   Take **wacky family polaroids** of yourselves in front of Sacramento landmarks: the Capitol building, Tower Bridge, the train station in Old Sac, etc. Make a photo collage and send it to someone who doesn't know how to use a smartphone.

364   **Take a German pit stop** to the German Deli on Auburn Blvd, and share a Bavarian Pretzel.

365   Indulge in the good-vibes with a **vegetarian sunflower burger** at Sunflower Drive In in Fair Oaks. Try a fruit smoothie too, and watch for friendly chickens roaming the property. Call in your order ahead for fast service on weekends. Take it to-go and eat it down the road at Plaza Park.

366   **Tune-up your bike** and add a practical (or silly) accessory at your nearest bike shop, like Velo Trap, Mike's Bikes, City Bicycles, or East Sac Bike Shop.

367   Take **competitive swimming to the next level with video analysis**, underwater filming and swim mirrors, & underwater photography at **Steve Wallen Swim School** in Folsom. Prices for underwater photography and videography start at $50, and it's available to the public, not just competitive swimmers. Makes a unique, special gift, and they also put together a short slide show for you!

368 Visit one of the many **amazing animal sanctuaries** we have in our region and meet some sweet, rescued animals with some amazing stories: Animal Place in Grass Valley, Animal Messenger Sanctuary in Sebastopol, Animal Sanctuary at Buena Vida Farm in Santa Rosa, Blackberry Creek Sanctuary in Colfax, California Potbellied Pigs Association in Pleasant Hill, Farm Sanctuary Northern California Shelter in Orland, NorCal Equine Rescue in Oroville, Piece of Peace Animal Sanctuary in Marysville, or Harvest Home Animal Sanctuary in Stockton.

369 Play hangman and blow bubbles at **McClatchy Park** in Oak Park. Walk to La Venadita and share some over-the-top nachos.

370   Go to **Black Friday Nights at the Folsom History Museum**, the first Friday of the month, 5-8pm, and gain access to the Pioneer Village after dark. Premium ticket holders ($30) get to **hammer on the forge** with supervision.

371   Rent or borrow a raft to launch at **River Bend Park**. Or just go for a picnic and explore its green, picturesque trails and spot some wild turkey and deer.

372   **Watch satellites orbiting the earth over Sacramento** at night. There are thousands of satellites circling the planet all the time. After sunset and through the night, you will be able to see dozens of them. They are reflected by the sun and move at a high velocity in the sky. How can you tell they are not a star? Stars "twinkle" because they are so far away and our atmosphere scatters their light. Satellites reflect the sun and are closer, so they move across the sky at a smooth, fast pace.

373   Let curious minds run loose at the **Carnival of Science** at the World of Wonders Science Museum in Lodi.

374   Play **bocce ball for free** at Sutter's Landing Park. Bring your own bocce balls. Bring your basketball too, if you want to run around and shoot some hoops on a kid-friendly half-court before leaving.

375   Teens in the 7th-9th grades can **tag along with a Sacramento Zoo keeper** for 3 hours and get a behind-the-scenes look at caring for wild and exotic animals. This program takes place a few times a year. Register early, $75.

376   Spend the morning at **Brooks Truitt Bark Park** on 19th & Q with your (or someone else's) dog. Take a peek at the flourishing community garden next door, complete with artichokes, giant sunflowers, and many varieties of lavender in the summertime.

377   **Write a letter to your representative** in Congress about an issue you care about and hand-deliver it to their Sacramento office. Call beforehand to try to ask if you can schedule a face-to-face meeting. Sometimes it works! Be persistent. *house.gov/representatives/find*

378   **Visit The Flower Farm** in Loomis in any season of the year for a special day playing on open grassy areas, weaving through vegetable gardens, being followed by exotic, fluffy chickens, and playing bocce ball near an inspiring nursery garden. Open every day except Tuesdays, closes at 4pm. Casque Wine Tastings 11am-5pm Thurs-Sun.

379   **Go on a sewer crawl** at the next Curby's Waste-a-Palooza and help Curby the recycling robot unclog pipes at the Utility Exploration Center's free family events in Roseville.

380   **Cheer on the California International Marathoners** on the steps of the State Capitol in December, and then grab some noodle soup to warm up at Ma Jong's across the street. See if the roses in the Rose Garden have been pruned yet.

381   Harmonize like a boss at the **Northern California Children's Chorus** in Roseville and Granite Bay. Mini-Glee workshop starts with K-2nd grade (no audition required) and singers can work all the way up to the Bella Voce group (high school), which recently performed at Carnegie Hall. One of their Summer Sing camps teaches songs from different cultures, in different languages, including French, Swahili, and Japanese. Includes outside recreation and crafts.

382   **Bend through a laser maze** untouched in the quickest amount of time, just like in the spy movies, at John's Incredible Pizza in Roseville. Then get your giggles out in the **bumper cars**.

383   **Eat lunch under a canopy of trees** at **Tower Cafe**. Avoid peak hours and weekends to get a good outdoor table. Bring pennies for the fountain. Next to the vintage Tower Theatre is Tower Pipes and Cigars, where you can get used wooden cigar boxes for $5 to decorate and use to store treasures.

384   See more than **1200 grinding holes in limestone**
       at **Indian Grinding Rock Loop Trails** (1.8-miles of
       connected loops), created by the Native American
       Miwok Indians for grinding foods like acorns to make
       acorn flower. Picnic grounds, fallen tree trunks,
       and open spaces make for a spectacular afternoon
       of exploration. What's more amazing is that you can
       actually camp there, in the regular campgrounds or
       in the cluster of 7 Miwok Indian bark huts (u'macha
       tam'ma) for up to 44 people. Experience a slice of
       Miwok life with your friends for $85/night (for *all* the
       bark huts)... though not for the faint of heart. Be sure
       not to miss the **2,000-3,000-year-old petroglyphs**.
       Near Pine Grove, CA. *parks.ca.gov* (Search Indian
       Grinding Rock, and scroll down to Environmental
       Living/Group Living.)

385   Discover exotic animals in a tropical forest setting at
       the **STAR Eco Station** in Rocklin. Guided tours start
       every hour on the hour.

386   Go for a hay ride, visit the farm animals, and get your
       fill of organic fruits and vegetables at **Sloan Winters
       Orchards** in Apple Hill, and take in the view.

387   Giddy up and take a **sunset trail horse ride** or
       an introductory lesson on horse riding at Shadow
       Glen Riding Stables in Fair Oaks or TLC Stables in
       Roseville.

388 **Get real-world experience in anchoring your climbing gear** on outdoor rocks with an expert on the **Quarry Trail** in Auburn. REI offers great introductory and advanced climbing classes. Ages 13 & up.

389 Find out why Rocklin used to be the "Granite Capitol of the West" at the cute, little **Rocklin History Museum**. Learn about Joel Parker Whitney, the wealthy rancher who is buried with 17 of his relatives in a pyramid tomb. (Secret hint: the pyramid is at the north end of Monument Park, 100 yards left of the 11th hole at Whitney Oaks Golf Course.)

390 Break the bustle of Thanksgiving morning and get out in the sunshine at the **Run To Feed The Hungry Walk/Run.**

391 Watch the annual traveling **Shen Yun show**, a Chinese cultural experience with dancing, storytelling, and beautiful folk traditions, which can't even be seen in China because the dance company says the Communist Party suppresses this type of traditional culture.

392 For strawberry fans, don't miss community-oriented **BerryFest** in Roseville in May, and get your tummies ready to fill with berries. There's also a car show, pageants, and live music at this two-day event at the Placer County Fairgrounds. *feedmeberries.com*

393   Watch a **free outdoor movie** during Gold Rush Days
      in September on the "1849 Scene," the grassy area in
      front of the California State Railroad Museum. Past
      movies have included western-inspired McClintock
      and Back to the Future III.

394   Rent a soccer ball at the Arden Creek Golf Course at
      Haggin Oaks and play some **FootGolf**. Golf hat and
      argyle socks not required, but look fantastic.

395   **Take a free trial Stroller Strides or Stroller Barre
      class** with Sacramento Fit4Mom. Playgroups after
      the Stroller Strides class take place weekly at Arden
      Park (Mondays), McKinley Park (Tuesdays), East Portal
      Parks (Wednesdays), and Land Park (Fridays).

396   **Take a dog for a treat at a dog bakery**, like Paws and
      the Palette in midtown.

397   Every second Saturday, visit the **Midtown Bizarre**,
      a happy little modern crafts market with live music,
      hosted by Identity Coffees on 28th St.

398   See the actual forearm and shin bone of a Apatosaurus
      (formerly known as Brontosaurus) from the Late
      Jurassic period – that's 150 million years old! The
      array of fossils and rare animals exhibits at the
      Natural Museum of History at Sierra College is
      astounding.

399   **Build a radio.** Get the parts you need at RC Country Hobbies on Folsom Blvd.

400   Play basketball on a trampoline, stumble through an obstacle course, or just jump around to your heart's content on dozens of trampolines at **Sky High Sports** in Rancho Cordova. Thursday night is Family Night, or take the littles ones to Munchkin Mondays.

401   Uncover the mystery of reading **tarot cards**, get some crystal stones, and learn all about your astrological sign at the tiny but packed spiritual shop Garden of Enchantment on 11th St. & K St. in Old Town. For older kids and teens.

402   Join the costume parade on a modern urban farm community at the **Autumn Harvest Festival** at The Cannery in Davis at the end of October.

403   Go to a Sacramento Public Library branch and find the **oldest newspaper** that they have on microfilm. Look at the pictures, headlines, and ads to find out what life was like back then. You're bound to find some pretty funny things!

404   A few times a year, talk about **other children in Sacramento who might need our help**, and what we can do. Check the "immediate needs" list of the **Children's Receiving Home of Sacramento** at their website, *crhkids.org*, and drop it off at their Auburn Blvd. location.

405   Bring a blanket and iced apple cider to **Fair Oaks Concerts** in the Park in July.

406   Get inspired by all the Californians that made history at the **California Museum**. View interactive exhibits on Native Americans, Remarkable Women, and a Constitutional Wall. Cool rotating exhibits too. Go on the first weekend of the month for free.

407   Get your hands dirty and learn about food and healthy eating at the one-hour Garden Fun for Children program in the **Read and Feed Training Program** at the Rancho Cordova Library. Every second and fourth Wednesday of the month, January through October.

408   The NCAA loves Sacramento. Find out which **college sports championships** Sacramento will be hosting from year to year and make plans early. We'll be hosting the Division I Cross Country Regional Championships in 2018 and 2021, the Division II Cross Country Championships in 2019, the Division I Track & Field Preliminary in 2022, and March Madness Basketball Championships in 2020.

409   Experiment with various oral poetic traditions and tell your story with **Lyricism 101** at the Boys & Girls Club Sacramento. Ages 13-18.

410   Visit **Seely Park's water park** daily in the summer between 10am-7pm.

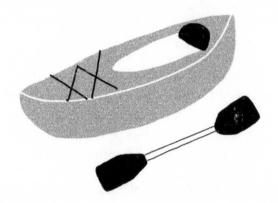

411   **Take a crew class** and glide across the water at
        Sacramento State Aquatic Center. Ages 12 & up.

412   Run some laps or **throw a football at Beaver
        Stadium** at American River College, one of the few
        stadiums open to the public in Sacramento.

413   **Fly paper airplanes** at your nearest park. Bring a
        hula hoop and take turns seeing who can get the most
        flights through the hoop. Use thick paper and master
        the Nakamura Lock. *sactownkids.com/paperplanes*

414   If you find yourselves in Auburn really wanting some
        pizza on a Saturday, stop by the **Foothills Farmers
        Market** for Scott Thorson's **mobile pizza show**
        through the window glass of his food truck, **Bella
        Familia**. For the smoky flavor, he uses pear, walnut,
        and apple tree trimmings.

415   **Get a booth near the fish tanks at Taro's** for some kid-friendly sushi and edamame beans. Stop by **Barnes & Noble** next door on your way out and check out the new books in the children's section.

416   Find a public swimming pool with a **twisty water slide**. *sactownkids.com/poolswithslides*

417   **Master a computer programming language** with Hours of Code, on Sacramento Public Library computers.

418   Take the toddlers on a **mini train ride** at the Fountains at Roseville, then share a pink lemonade or chocolate almond drink at the fire pit, and then throw pennies in the fountain. In the summer, wear swim suits and cool off at the splash pad.

419   See the tiny, but very old **Cactus Garden in Capitol Park**, just south of the rose garden. Some of the plants were donated by schoolchildren in 1914, making them over 100 years old. Indoors, cacti can survive for one or two decades, but in the wild they can live for hundreds of years!

420   Cool off at a **water sprayground next to a playground** for double the fun, like the Stephenson Family Park in Elk Grove or McClatchy Playground in Oak Park.

421   Find out when the **Sacramento Ballet** is having their next Second Saturday **open studio**. Be captivated by the beauty of dancers practicing up close with excerpts and commentary on their current performance.

422   Grab a refreshing, kid-friendly **fresh-pressed juice** like beet lemonade or organic watermelon strawberry freeze at Sun & Soil Juice Company on P & 19th. Walk 3 blocks to enjoy it in front of the fountain at Fremont Park.

423   Ride the Crazy Dane **roller coaster** at night at Scandia Fun Center.

424   Plan a Sunday brunch for a special occasion at **Grand Island Mansion** in Walnut Grove, the largest private estate in Northern California.

425   Find out how to build an **easy DIY composting bin** from Sacramento-based *wormfancy.com's* website, and then order their worm castings to get started. More than 50% of household waste in California is organic material that could be composted. Instead they fill up landfills, where they likely emit methane into the earth's atmosphere.

426   Start small with your **skateboarding tricks** at the (relatively) shallow skate bowl at Morse Park in Elk Grove.

427   Soak up some Sacramento history from a boat captain on a fun, hour-long **Hornblower** river cruise.

428   Join the **Dinger's Kid Club with the Sacramento River Cats** minor league baseball team and participate in exclusive pre-game activities. Past activities have included VIP ballpark tour, taking a pitch from a River Cats player in a whiffle pre-game, playing catch on the field before the game, VIP player autograph session, being a guest PA for one inning, and game ball delivery. ($10 per child, 12 & under)

429   **Ice skate in charming, historic Folsom**. A circular ice rink surrounds a towering Christmas tree on the railroad turn stop. Walk a couple blocks to nourish and hydrate with a 'Creamsicle' juice (apple, carrot, orange, coconut water, and vanilla bean) at Pure Life Juice Company, or get a special treat at Karen's Bakery.

430   Game, set, match. Play some **hard court tennis** on one of McKinley Park's eight, lighted, well-maintained tennis courts.

431   Taste 40 different flavors of **homemade fudge made fresh daily** at the Fudge Factory Farm in Camino. They are also a sustainable family run organic farm with a cute, little kids play area and alpacas you can visit, right next to High Hill Ranch.

432   Feel the mesmerizing **Western African drumming beats** at Fenix Drum and Dance's next event.

433   Share secrets in the semi-secret **WPA Rock Garden in Land Park**, an enchanting little garden with cobble-stoned steps and wooded fences. Play a game of tag or hide-and-seek to get the full experience.

434   Wakeboard, paddle board, or do some safe beach swimming at the enclosed **Wake Island Waterpark** in Pleasant Grove, 15 minutes from Sacramento. Kids under 48" are free.

435   Hit up the **Pacific Rim Street Fest** in Southside Park in May, and eat while enjoying cultural activities, crafts, and live music. Free.

436   **Work as a family to solve a mystery** and get out of the escape room at **Enchambered** on Arden Way. Recommended for ages 9 & up. Request their most family-friendly room.

437   Run down the wooded trail at **Waterton Access** off of La Riviera Drive (or the nearby S.A.R.A. Access). See if you can find **spot a giant jack rabbit**, deer, or coyote.

438   Trot down to the annual **Sacramento Farm-to-Fork Festival** in September, where local producers showcase where our local food comes from, with A-list sponsors, cooking demonstrations, interactive booths, and a kids' zone. Free.

439   Reserve your spot early for the **Valentine's Drop-Off Night at the Museum**, so kids can play in their pajamas, make arts and crafts at the **Sacramento Children's Museum**, while adults enjoy a child-free romantic evening.

440   **Rent an RV for a weekend** (Happy Daze RV, El Monte RV, Advantage Caravans) and venture deep into a forest or tiny lakeside campground where there are no hotels or shopping malls and kids run wild and free in nature. Or cruise on down to Carmel Beach or Santa Cruz on whim. Some specials start at $100/night on the off-season.

441   Customize your own bear at **Build-A-Bear Workshop** at Galleria at Roseville.

442   Take a trip around the world at the **iFest** in May in Rancho Cordova. Non-stop cultural performances by **Irish, Indian, Filipino, Hawaiian, and other dancers** are joined by food trucks, and worldly arts and crafts. Recent activities have included Ukrainian egg art, African drumming, henna tattoos, piñatas, and kite demonstrations. Free.

443   Build a pontoon or a skyscraper at **Lego Mania**, a monthly, one-hour activity at various Sacramento Public Libraries. Check *saclibrary.org's* event listings for the next one at your local library. Lego bricks provided.

444   Take the little ones to **"Tots on the Tee"** at Haggin Oaks Golf Course and let them practice their eye-hand coordination with other budding golfers. Ages 3-4.

445   Taste the sweetness of summer at the **Woodland Tomato Festival** in August.

446   Take a water polo clinic at **El Dorado Hills Aquatic Center**. Ages 8-12.

447   Try some sweet potato ice cream and sweet potato pie at the annual **Sweet Potato Festival**, hosted by the Sacramento Valley Section of National Council of Negro Women Inc. in February.

448   Go on **Underground Tour**, starting at the Sacramento History Museum, and see the original stores and markets that Sacramento was literally built on in the 1860s. Ages 6-17.

449   Dive into thousands of strands of beads, gems, crystals, minerals, and fossils at the **Gem Faire** at the Scottish Rite Center. They usually take place at least four times a year.

450   Wake up early during the summer months and **go to a u-pick farm** to pick your own strawberries, blackberries, pears... bring sunscreen and a hat! Find a u-pick farm near Sacramento at *pickyourown.org* and call ahead.

451 Watch seasoned actors perform live at the **Sacramento Community Theatre**.

452 Wear green and white and watch a **women's volleyball game** at Sacramento State.

453 Discover the **mystery of vernal pools** at Mather Field. Vernal pools are rare ecosystems that flood in the winter and completely dry up in the spring. The vernal pools are over 50,000 years old and contain more than 200 plant species, many that are not found anywhere else. Public tours available during the flowering and wet phases. Flower Walks and Critter Walks also available. *sacsplash.org*

454 Visit the **nature-themed playground** at Bannon Creek park in South Natomas. Coast along the easy 1.17-mile bike trail ride.

455 Any ball, any wall. Sign up for **Youth Handball Play** every first Sunday at Sacramento Turn Verein and learn the rules of this versatile game. Ages 6 & up.

456 Hear little angel voices sing surprisingly complex pieces at the **Sacramento Children's Chorus'** next performance. Kids workshops and choir groups start at Kindergarten, if you have a little songbird in the family.

457   Pinch, coil, and throw some clay on a wheel at the
        Kids & Clay weekly class at Alpha Fired Arts. 1st
        grade & up.

458   Walk, bike, or carpool to the downtown **Earth Day
        Festival** in April. Make a pledge to up your family
        recycling game this year, plant a tree, and cut back on
        bottled water. And remember, when you throw away,
        it's never really "away."

459   See Israeli dancers move to the beat and enjoy some
        Jewish food at the **Jewish Heritage Festival** in April/
        May. Face-painting and bounce houses make it fun for
        the little ones.

460   **Practice your skee-ball** and air hockey skills at
        Chuck E. Cheese in Sacramento (and check out their
        $7.49 lunch buffet) or Dave & Busters in Roseville,
        which has a full restaurant.

461   Take a beginner **speed skating** lesson at Roller King
        Roseville. $10. Helmet required, not included.

462   **See the next puppet show** at Fairytale Town. When
        you get home, make a tension rod stage curtain at
        home between a doorway and perform your own
        puppet show for the family.

463   **Rent an e-book for free** from the Sacramento Public
        Library's digital library. *saclibrary.org/Digital-Library*

464   Stain your fingers pink at **Patrick's U-Pick Berry Farm** in Camino during berry season in the summertime. Picnic in the shade, look for squash blossoms, and praying mantis – the natural pest control boss.

465   **Take a mini, small-scale steam train ride** on weekends at the Sacramento Valley Live Steamers Railroad Museum, located within the **Hagan Community Park** in Rancho Cordova. Check their calendar for special kid-friendly events.

466   Teens with dance experience can experiment with **contemporary and modern dance** and choreography at the Hawkins School of Performing Arts in Folsom.

467   Visit the West Sacramento community of Bridgeway, where the **"Main Drain" garden** will delight the senses, with its tricycle and chandelier art hanging from tree branches. Cozy up to a book out of the free little library box and share a picnic on the hand-painted picnic tables.

468   Fill the shoes of a scientist, engineer, or mathematician on **board the International Space Station** in a Simulated Micronaut Mission at the Powerhouse Science Center. Find out when their next mission date is taking place. Ages 4-8 with participating adult.

469   **Skip along the river walk**, watching the boats, ducks, and geese go by. See if you can identify which ducks and geese you see. *(sactownkids.com/birds)* Then **share a fancy, vegetable lasagna or portobello reuben sandwich** at **Ten22** in Old Town Sacramento.

470   Wanna dance to drums and do acrobatics and martial arts all at once? Discover **Capoeira,** a fun and unique African-Brazilian tradition that will have you looking at dancing in a whole new light. This type of dance melds West African music and movement to the distinct cultural traditions of colonial Brazil.

471   Get the kids out of the house Sunday morning for the best fruit and vegetable picks at the **Elk Grove Farmers Market** 8am-noon at Old Town Plaza. Then take your bounty to eat at the nearby **Rain Garden Plaza**, a tiny park that acts as a living laboratory that includes bio filtration swales and water harvesting features. It's the first comprehensive, large-scale rain garden in California educating citizens on sustainable water practices and native, drought-resistant plants.

472   Experiment with **bluegrass and folk on the dobro** (or other guitars) with Kathy Barwick. She trains you to master recorded solos by ear, create your own arrangements, and improvise. Recommended for teens. *kathybarwick.net*

473   **Watch the next moonrise in Sacramento** and find out what direction and degree it will be in the sky. Kids love to find and follow the moon.
https://www.timeanddate.com/moon/usa/sacramento

474   **Take a picture of an unusual bug** and try to identify the species. If you can't figure it out, take your picture to the UC Davis Bohart Museum of Entomology (also a working lab) and see if a scientist there can identify it and tell you all about it.

475   Celebrate with a blueberry donut at the **old-fashioned, cult-favorite Marie's Donuts.** They start baking every night at 11pm! Closes at 4pm.

476   Take up the **Mountain Shredders** program at Sugar Bowl ski resort, and take your skiing/snowboarding to the next level. Ages 6 & up.

477 Go to the next **basket weaving demonstration** at the State Indian Museum, where native weavers explain their techniques and materials and how they plan the artistic construction. Free with admission.

478 Have a family **basketball shoot-out** at an outdoor basketball court, like tree-covered William Land Park or the wide-open and clean courts at Morse Park in Elk Grove.

479 **Get certified in babysitter training** with the American Red Cross in Sacramento and discover how to care for kids and babies, and what to do in an emergency situation. Ages 11 & up.

480 **Rollerblade** or take an easy stroll down the paved walking trails at the William B. Pond Recreation Area.

481 Why wait for a camp-out? **Make s'mores** at your favorite Sacramento park with a self-lighting log on a picnic grill. Almost all parks have a grill, thank goodness.

482 **Start a rock collection** at Ology, a rock shop tucked into a tiny space in Old Town at 130 K St. See and touch hundreds of rocks, crystals, gemstones, fossilized bones, and petrified wood too. Boxes are stacked high and the space is cramped, so have an idea of what you want to see, and don't be afraid to ask for assistance.

483   Explore the worlds of electricity, magnetism, and physics at the **World of Wonders Science Museum** in Lodi. Bring a friend for free every last Friday of the month. Make a day of it and also visit **Fun Town** and **Wortley Lake** at Micke Grove Regional Park.

484   Go to the **Dinosaur Day Science Fest** in May at Sierra College's Museum of Natural History. Past events have included a polymer ooze booth, exploding watermelons, glow-in-the-dark bacterial art, DIY Archaeopteryx hats, make your own Cartesian diver, and a real set of lungs that you can see fill with air.

485   In February, enter and run the Super Sunday Run for a 10k, 5k, 1k, or the super-cute **Pee-Wee 40-Yard Dash** for toddlers. Starts and finishes at the Sac State campus, with the final festivities in the Hornets stadium. Get a gorgeous view of the school's campus, the Guy West Bridge, and windy tree-lined roads.

486   Pile on the love for Mother Earth on Mother's Day weekend in May at the annual **Whole Earth Festival** in Davis, a celebration with food, crafts, and educational booths run by UC Davis students.

487   Scream your way down **7-story near-vertical free-fall** drop in 8 seconds, experiencing the powerful cling of G-Forces, at Golfland SunSplash. Must be 48".

488   Share a **bright-pink acai bowl** (berry smoothie in a bowl) at **Vibe Health Bar** for energy and then walk to McClatchy Park's swimming pool and practice your dives off the low diving board. Kinds can bounce around the playground and watch teens do tricks on the skate ramp.

489   Join the youth climbing club at **Granite Arch** and discover new ways to become a better climber.

490   Hang out in the lofty, 5-story atrium of Wells Fargo Center (400 Capitol Mall), home to the free Wells Fargo History Museum. **See a real stagecoach** from the mid-1800's, real gold specimens, a working telegraph line, and watch video presentations of the Gold Rush that started in California in 1849. Share a scoop of raspberry sorbet at Il Fornaio restaurant on the ground floor on your way out.

491   Play flag football in the wintertime with the **youth indoor flag football league** at Olympus Sports Coliseum.

492   See a funny kid-friendly musical at the 120-year old **Woodland Opera House**, a California State Historic Landmark.

493   Sit down for **storytime with puppets and wild animals** at Folsom Zoo Sanctuary every fourth Thursday of the month.

494   Take your bikes to **ride the Davis Bike Loop** and rest at nice, quiet parks along the way, like Willowcreek Park. Bring a book to read on breaks.

495   Watch professional jumpers, the U.S. Navy Blue Angels, and Bomber planes get into formation at the **California Capitol Airshow** in October. Don't miss the Launchpad where kids can learn about aerospace innovations, space artifacts, robotics, a fly simulator, and other STEM activities. Toddlers especially love the Hangar exhibit with bouncy inflatables, put together by the Sacramento Children's Museum.

496   Play **horseshoes** at one of the four horseshoe courts at the Western-themed Horseshoe Park in Elk Grove. Bring your own horseshoes and country sass.

497   **Let the kids eat with their hands** at the Ethiopian restaurant Queen Sheba on Broadway. They'll love that bread is used as a napkin!

498   **Watch pizza dough being thrown into the air**, and piping-hot pizzas coming out of the brick ovens at Hot Italian or Pizza Rock.

499   Check out the next **"Hands on History"** event at Sutter's Fort and discover trades from the 1800s like trapping and blacksmithing, write with quill and ink, and watch how flint and steel can be used to start a fire.

500 Meet local artisans, do some kids' activities, listen to live music, and snack at food trucks at the annual **Curtis Fest** at the end of August.

501 Blow some bubbles and have a summer picnic on the grassy area of the **Old Sugar Mill**, where adults can taste wine from a dozen different local wineries. Dog-friendly (on leash) and open every day 11am-5pm, except Thanksgiving, Christmas, and New Year's Day. Just 15 minutes from Sacramento.

502 Master basic rowing techniques and the value of teamwork at the **River City Rowing Club** in West Sacramento. Ages 10 & up.

503 Get a **free roller skating lesson** at The Rink 9:30-10:30 am every Saturday, with paid session ($5).

504 Get a vivid, colorful kite from **Old City Kites** in Old Sacramento, and take it to the skies.

505 Catch a **free movie in the park** at Central Park in Davis on Saturday nights at sunset during the summer, hosted by the Rotary Club.

506 **Use a real telegraph**, dress up as a railroad messenger, and watch "The Shrinking World" silent movie at the Old Sacramento Wells Fargo History Museum on 2nd Street in the historic Hastings Building, where Wells Fargo opened it's second office in 1854.

507 **Pick your own strawberries and blackberries** in the summertime at **Pacific Star Gardens** u-pick farm on County Road 99 in Woodland. This is a self-serve, honor-system, Yolo County Certified Organic farm. Bring cash, with small bills for exact change. Follow them on Facebook for updates.

508 Go on the next **Nature Trail Guided Walk** of the **Consumnes River Preserve** where naturalists guide families through the oak woodlands and describe the surrounding wildlife and botanicals. This interactive tour during nice weather season is perfect for little inquiring minds.

509 Play on a playground in 1.5 feet of water at **Pee Wee Splash'n Play** in Elk Grove. $5 admission, 8 & under. Babies under 1 and adults free.

510 **Make a flowerbomb** of wildflower seeds and give a little love to a bare corner of your Sacramento neighborhood. *sactownkids.com/flowerbomb*

511 Take aspiring modern dancers to the next **open rehearsals at Core Contemporary Dance**.

512 Plan an overnight trip to Tahoe around the **Lakeview Commons Summer Concert Music Series**. Lakeview Commons at El Dorado Beach is the largest beach area in South Lake Tahoe. Spend the day in the swim area, on the bike trails, or kayaking on the water.

513 Drive north on Mace Blvd in northeast Davis, where it turns into East Covell Blvd, and see a **sea of blooming sunflowers** in the summer.

514 **Write your very own book** and watch copies being printed right before your very own eyes at the Espresso Book Machine at Sacramento Public Library's Central branch, only one of two EBM machines available in California. ($25 for set-up, $6 per book, 3-cents per page. Pricing is approximately $45 for three 25-page books. *saclibrary.org*

515 Take a free **Armenian circle dance** lesson at the **Armenian Food Festival** in October. Eat some stuffed grape leaves, hummus, pilaf, and Armenian Mac & Cheese. See instrumentalists play traditional West Asian music on wind and string instruments, like the duduk, an Armenian apricot wood flute.

516 Get some tap shoes and **tap the day away** at Tricks Gymnastics, Dance, and Swim in Sacramento, Folsom, and Granite Bay. Kids can also take ballet, jazz, hip hop, and more. Baby gym classes start at just 10 weeks old, a perfect morning out of the house for new moms.

517 Go on a two-hour, kid-friendly Vernal Pool **Flower Walk** with scientists in April at Mather Field. Register early as this event sells out.

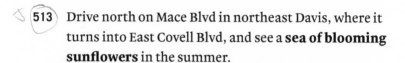

518   In March, throw your fishing pole into the **Annual Trout Fishing Derby** at Howe Park Pond. Advance household admission $18 gets in five family members. All ages are welcome, but participants older than 16 need a fishing license.

519   Play on a real **wooden playground** with real tire obstacle courses surrounded by oak trees at the beautiful **Folsom Kids Play Park**, on Prewitt Drive in Folsom.

520   Go on a carnival ride, watch a talent competition, and see some monster trucks at the **Sacramento County Fair** in May. Free for kids 12 & under.

521   **Master safe biking in the city.** Take a 90-minute **Urban Bicycling 101** class with the City of Sacramento. It's free, but each class fills up in advance so register early for their next class, held every second Thursday of the month. Learn how to navigate complicated situations on the road and avoid crashes. For teens with a parent.

522   Experience what it feels like to fall through the sky with **indoor skydiving** at iFly in Roseville. Ages 3 & up.

523   Watch some Brazilian dancing and move to the beat at the summer **Annual Brazilian Festival**.

524   Go to Land Park and **collect pine cones** for the holidays. Scent with pure cinnamon oil, apply glue on the edges and sprinkle with gold glitter.

525   **See an iron lung**, live leeches, glass eyes, a skeleton, ancient x-ray machines, and other fascinating artifacts at the **Museum of Medical History in Sacramento**. Free admission, open M-F and some Saturdays on special national museum days.

526   Spend the morning at geese-lovin' McKinley Park in East Sacramento and take a **spin on the giant (but slow) merry-go-round**. Parents can pick up a drink at one of the many nearby indie coffeehouses: Pachamama, Coffee Works, Chocolate Fish, Tiferet, or Tupelo.

527   **Bowl the night away** at your favorite bowling alley, like Country Club Lanes, Capital Bowl, AMF Land Park Lanes, or Pins N Strikes. Look for special family events like **"glow bowling."**

528   Teens can become a City of Sacramento volunteer and help out with programs like **Access Leisure**, which provides social activities for the elderly. Past events include a game of Goalball, which is a sport designed for the blind and visually impaired. It was originally created for War veterans who lost their sight in World War II. You can help referee, retrieve balls, set-up, and tear-down. Ages 14 & up.

529   Head south to the **Lodi Lake Nature Trail** a paved nature trail perfect for strollers, just 2.5-miles long. Wild Himalayan blackberries flank the trail, along some areas. You'll see lots of cottonwood and huge Valley oaks, as well as little critters ranging from frogs to hummingbirds to pond turtles. The nearby Lodi Lake Discovery Museum is a natural history museum with free admission.

530   **Make some doll clothes** with silky velvet, lace, buttons, and trim at **Hi-Fashion Fabrics** on Franklin Blvd.

531   Travel back in time and share a sorbet, classic ice cream sundae, or banana split at an old-fashioned ice cream parlor like **Vic's**, **Gunther's, or Leatherby's**.

532   **Roll down a hill overlooking the apple orchards** in autumn at Delfino Farm. Dig in to a French apple pie and feed the chickens.

533 Find out when **Hacker Lab** on I St. is having their next open house, and tour the inside of a cool makerspace for artists who are using innovative tools and technology to make new things. Occasionally, they offer programs for teens, check listings.

534 **Get a helmet-fitting** at the next bicycle safety inspection at the annual **Bike Fest** in Roseville. Fun obstacle courses and riding demonstrations run all day for the kids.

535 Take train enthusiasts to **The Great Train Show** at Cal Expo in January, and peruse hundreds of tables of trains, do kids activities, and stop by educational exhibits. Kids 11 & under are free.

536 Special needs children can qualify for a scholarship to receive twelve 30-minute horse riding lessons at **Horses for Healing**, a volunteer-run organization in Auburn for people with physical, psychological, and emotional disabilities.

537 Go to your favorite Sacramento park and make **gigantic bubbles** for the kids to chase. Make a homemade giant bubble maker out of sticks and string. *sactownkids.com/projects*

538 See the delicate, pale, confetti-like **cherry blossoms** bloom in spring at Belle Cooledge Park.

539 Take older kids to the one-hour **Leave No Trace Awareness Workshop** and camp at Camp Pollock for free. They'll learn how to minimize their impact in the great outdoors, best methods for interacting with wildlife, and tips for leaving no trace at home and in the community. *sacramentovalleyconservancy.org*

540 Spend the morning experiencing the three pillars of Native California life: Nature, Spirit, Family, at the **State Indian Museum** on K street. See a real hand-carved canoe, ceremonial beadwork, and hunting and fishing tools more than 2400 years old!

541 **Go to a barn dance** in Apple Hill in August. The annual Camino Barn Dance is usually held at Rainbow Orchards and benefits community programs in Camino.

542 **See a $1 movie** at Regal Cinemas on Wednesdays. Follow it up with a $1 Wednesday frozen yogurt at Big Spoon.

543 Go on a Sunday drive through the **Sacramento Delta**, get a picnic lunch in Clarksburg, and enjoy the view of farmlands, colorful barns, and the cool Delta breeze.

544 For a water **spray park with a fantastic view** of gold rolling hills, visit **Promontory Community Park** in El Dorado Hills, open Memorial Day weekend to Labor Day weekend.

545   Go **trout fishing** (hook and release) at Indian Rock Tree Farm.

546   Drop in to a family-friendly matinee performance at the cute and quaint **Sutter Street Theatre** in Folsom.

547   **Transport to the tropics** and visit an Asian food market (like Ranch 99, SF Market, Asian Food Center) and pick out some juicy exotic fruit like mangoes, lychee, persimmon, papayas, and coconuts and have a tropical fruit party. Get a coconut opening tool and drink some young coconuts. Scoop out the sweet, creamy insides for dessert.

548   Play a round of **mini golf** at Scandia Fun Center at 11am when crowds are thin, and try to hit a hole in one.

549   Organize a **watercolor party** along the American River. Bring a blanket, a few bottles of water, bowls, paintbrushes, watercolor paints, and good, thick, hardy paper.

550   Pick up a disposable camera with real film and let the kids take pictures of what your typical day looks like, in 24 exposures. Then take it to Photosource on Elvas Avenue for some **good, old-fashioned photo printing**. Pick out their favorite to enlarge and frame.

551 Walk around a **3-acre miniature city** where everything is kid-sized, including the fire department and post office. Safetyville, USA in Rancho Cordova hosts several fun family events a year, including Free Family Bike Nights, Taste of the Little City in May, Family Day in June, and the Annual Halloween Haunt in October.

552 Go on a **wilderness raft trip** with a tour group, like Tributary Whitewater Tours, and ride along a Class II rafting run on the Lower Middle Fork of the American River in Gold Country. Ages 4 & up.

553 See the 1200+ daylily varieties, ducks, frogs, and 300-year old Heritage Oak trees at the incredible **Amador Flower Farm**, one hour southeast of Sacramento in the Sierra Foothills. Get fixings for a picnic at the nearby Amador Vintage Market beforehand. Open daily in the spring, summer, and fall 9-4pm. Open Thursday through Sunday in the winter. Free, but you can reserve a picnic table for $5 during the peak season.

554 Help Oroville **celebrate the thousands of salmon making their long journey** from the ocean back up to their birthplace in Feather River at the annual, family-friendly **Oroville Salmon Festival** in September. Free and includes environmental education, tour of the hatchery, food trucks, and live music.

555   **Have a Mediterranean picnic** at your favorite park, after picking up some Greek falafels at **Opa! Opa!**. Feelin' more like a middle eastern/Moroccan falafel? Try **Cafe Morocco** on Alhambra Blvd. Or complete your falafel quest at **Falafel and Planet Shwarma**, our favorite middle eastern falafel in town, on Florin Rd, next to 99 Ranch Asian market. Our kids love the grape leaf rolls, pita bread, hummus, and babaghanoush.

556   Wheel around a kid-sized grocery cart at **Trader Joe's** or **Sacramento Natural Foods Co-op**. Don't forget to get a sticker!

557   **Donate some of your favorite non-perishable food items** and canned goods to a food bank that serves less fortunate families, like Sacramento Food Bank and Family Services, El Dorado Family Food Bank, Yolo Food Bank, Twin Lakes Food Bank, Elk Grove Food Bank, and River City Food Bank.

558   **Play bananagrams** in a tiny urban park with a community garden like Zapata Park in the Alkali Flat area of downtown.

559   Bring your cherry pitter to the **Linden Cherry Festival** in May. Truckloads of fresh cherries, live bands, and games for the kids.

560   Take some friends to **play bingo** at Sacramento Bingo Center.

561   Got a little one bouncing off walls? Put them on a trampoline. Go to the morning **Toddler Time at Sky Zone** in Rocklin. Older kids love to bounce too, and of course, most adults.

562   Personally **thank the veterans** you know and then honor them at the annual City of Sacramento Veterans Day Parade in November as military organizations, marching bands, and community organizations march down the Capitol Mall. Look up street closures and plan your route in advance.

563   Slide down the 140-foot water slide called Clyde's Plunge at the **Jerry Fox Swim Center** in Elk Grove. Enjoy a fudge bar at Clyde's Cave snack bar. Under 2 free, 2-4 $1, 5 & older $3.

564   Pay homage to Johnny Cash (he sang "Folsom Prison Blues") and ride your scooter to the upcoming 3-acre **Johnny Cash Legacy Park** along the Johnny Cash Trail in Folsom. A public art walk is planned and will feature eight larger-than-life pieces, including a 40-foot steel sculpture of Cash, a "Ring of Fire" made of giant red guitar picks arranged in a 12-foot tall circle, 17-foot high steel guitar necks, and two 7-foot black bronze guitar picks. The park connects to Johnny Cash Bridge, modeled after the East gate tower at Folsom prison. Check park's website for progress updates.

565 Bring fixings for sandwiches or burritos and **picnic at the beautiful, riverfront Garcia Bend Park** in Sacramento's Pocket neighborhood. Run around the playground or bring a soccer ball and tennis racquets for some fun competition.

566 **Practice cartwheels** or blow bubbles at tiny Winn Park on P St. Cross the street to get some sushi and miso soup at Lou's Sushi, or walk a block to Suzie Burger.

567 Get emotionally centered with **Tai Chi, Tae Kwon Do, or Karate** in a beginner's class at various City of Sacramento recreation centers.

568 Behold whimsical clay works at the annual **California Clay Competition at The Artery** in Davis.

569 Take a **kids golf clinic** at Ancil Hoffman Park public golf course.

570 Watch your white shirt glow-in-the-dark at **Monster Mini Golf** in Rancho Cordova.

571 Give the kids a taste of the past and **peruse old baseball cards and old-school comic books** at small, hole-in-the-wall hobby shops like H R Sports Cards and Collectibles on 10th St., Broadway Comics and Cards on Broadway, Teammates in Carmichael, or California Card Company in Elk Grove.

572 Go hiking around **Rossmoor Bar**, a peninsula surrounded on all three sides by the American River in Rancho Cordova. Watch rafters tackle the San Juan Rapids, a challenging Class II area.

573 **Tee up at the larger-than-life mini golf courses** at Golfland SunSplash in Roseville: Course #1 Adventure Golf or Course #2 Lost Continent.

574 **Get photographed** in your Halloween costume for free at a special photo session by **Naomi Harrison Photography**, benefiting Loaves and Fishes, a non-profit helping homeless families. Just bring a pack of diapers to donate. Kids love Naomi, and her bright, exquisite photos beg to be framed. *naomiharrisonphotography.com*

575 Play basketball with younger kids on the **shorter, lowered basketball hoop at McClatchy Park** in the Oak Park neighborhood.

576 **Donate all the fancy dresses** and men's formal wear you can to the Sacramento Public Library's Prom Drive to help teens in need. Especially menswear!

577 Experience traditional Russian culture, food, dance, music, and arts and crafts at the annual **Russian Festival** in downtown Sacramento. Previous events have been in September at the Holy Ascension Church. Kids 12 & under free.

578 Watch youth and high school **lacrosse** games with the Sacramento Fall League on Sundays at Mather Sports Complex. Seventh graders can sign up to play in the summer.

579 Record a video of yourself performing your favorite song and send it in to **Sac's Got Talent** in September, for a chance to perform in their October show. *kidshelpingkidssac.org*

580 See some **stunning street art** at the annual **Chalk It Up!** In September. Food and craft vendors make this a bona fide art party.

581 Watch dance majors present their original works at the **Sacramento State Senior Dance Concert** at the end of spring semester in May. $5-12. *csus.edu/dram*

582 Take budding gardeners on a daytrip to the **National Heirloom Exposition** in Santa Rosa. The "celebration of pure food" is the largest display of heritage food in the world, with unique and funky varieties on display.

583 Stop by to look at pretty cookies and cakes at **Freeport Bakery**, especially around Valentine's Day or Christmas.

584 Listen to live **jazz and blues** at a family-friendly café that serves food, like Luna Café.

585   **Get your personal finances off to a good start** at a
       local credit union like Golden 1 or Sacramento Credit
       Union and open a savings account.

586   Pick up some **sports tricks** by watching a competitive
       high school game. For the current schedule, go to:
       http://www.kcra.com/high-school-sports

587   Meet award-winning children's book authors from
       around the country, and listen to them read their own
       books at the annual **ScholarShare Children's Book
       Festival** at Fairytale Town in September.

588   In the late springtime, hike with older kids to the
       120-foot **Bassi Falls** in Pollock Pines, 4 miles out and
       back. By late summer, most of the water has receded,
       so be sure to do this hike by early summer. For double
       the fun, camp at the nearby Ice House Reservoir
       campgrounds.

589   Wander downtown and **find all of artist Gale Hart's darts and dart game pieces** around the Golden1 Center (runs along L St. between 5th & 7th St.). Then, see if you can make out the piglet in Jeff Koons "Coloring Book #4," an 18-foot tall chrome sculpture at Golden1 Center, part of his Celebration series, which was inspired by the artist's fascination with "childhood experiences and optimistic consciousness." Don't miss the immersive sound experience by artist Bill Fontana, and try to find all 34 small loudspeakers in the planters and on the green living walls in the plaza on the north side of the arena.

590   Check out the Kids' Zone at the **California State Capitol Museum**, and see where the laws of the land are made. Take the elevator to the 6th floor to grab a bite at the new Statehouse Café.

591   **Watch a jousting tournament** and 16th century cultural re-enactments at the kid-friendly Folsom Renaissance Faire, usually held in September.

592   Discover **advanced painting and drawing techniques** at a Material Explosion session at Crocker Art Museum. Ages 7-12.

593   Get some lumpy, bumpy, and **gorgeous u-pick organic pumpkins** in October at the certified organic 24Carrot Farm in Apple Hill.

594   See a fantastically funny, family-friendly play by the **Roseville Theatre Arts Academy**. Or take a theatre workshop at the non-profit and get an inside look at behind-the-scenes workings of a play. Ages 4 & up.

595   Pack your swimsuit and go **"resort camping"** at the Tahoe Valley Campground near Lake Tahoe. This privately run camp has a tennis, pickleball, basketball, volleyball, a playground, heated swimming pool in the summer, nice showers, laundry, a trolley station, and a clubhouse.

596   Eat a pancake breakfast and participate in a fun run and other kid-focused activities at the annual **Fair Oaks Fiesta** at Fair Oaks Village in May.

597   **Interested in law?** See what it's like to work in the DA's office. High school sophomores and juniors are invited to apply to the **District Attorney Youth Academy** where they will meet twice a month during the school year to delve into topics like: anatomy of a criminal case, laboratory of forensic science, crime scene investigation (CSI). A one-day field trip takes the kids on a tour of the Sacramento Superior Court. *sacda.org*

598   Test drive and **find out all about electric cars** at the Sacramento International Auto Show in October at Cal Expo.

599 Use your Sacramento Public Library account to **master conversational basics in more than 70 languages** through their Mango Language online learning program and track you progress.

600 Find **Oops C Daisy & Hugz**, a dynamic clown duo, at events open to the public through their Facebook page.

601 Get ready for bed and jump in the car for **Pajama Storytime** at Folsom Public Library on Tuesdays at 7pm. All ages welcome, bring your favorite stuffed animal, pillow, or blanket.

602 Clap and thump along with the internationally recognized **Sacramento Mandarins Drum and Bugle Corps** at one of their community events. Or if you're a passionate drummer, audition to join them! Since 1963, they've won eight Drum Corps International World Championship Titles.

603 Identify Sacramento area trees and do leaf rubbings on the free **Fall Colors Walk** at Effie Yeaw Nature Center in November. Naturists and guides are on-hand to educate you on the special lives of trees.

604 Watch a **hockey game** or take a beginner's hockey class at Skatetown in Roseville or Norcal Indoor Sports in Woodland.

605   Take a **beginner's piano lesson** and learn some easy songs with the Sacramento City Parks and Recreation.

606   Watch some head-spinning dance routines at the **Headliners Regional Dance Competition** in Sacramento, usually in April.

607   Take a fun **Candlelight Tour of Sutter's Fort** in November, and experience pioneer life lit by candles after dark.

608   Delight in classic children's performances at budget-friendly prices ($8) at the **Chautauqua Playhouse** in the La Sierra Community Center in Carmichael.

609   Get a custom song on any subject you like for $5 at the **one-man music show in a little van**, the Acoustic Sanctuary, anytime after 7:30pm on Thursday through Saturday on the corner of 22nd & J St. Winko Ljizz plays a baby grand piano and a myriad of other instruments in the tiniest of spaces. He does not disappoint, and you can stay as long as you want.

610   Learn about the wonderful world of string instruments at the Sacramento Institute for Music and the Arts summer camp. Ages 6 & up. *sacima.org*

611   **Play laser tag for $5** a game on Freak Out Wednesdays at Lasertag of Carmichael.

612   **Borrow an accordion, thumb piano, rain stick**, electric guitar, or any of the other 200+ instruments at the Library of Musiclandria. Free with a library card.

613   Take a **clay sculpture class** and let your imagination run wild at **Alpha Fired Arts**. There are a variety of kids classes, camps, and programs. Teens can sometimes take advanced classes with an adult, with prior approval.

614   **Watch thousands of graceful Sand Hill Cranes** descend on the region's beautiful grasslands and marshes at the **Lodi Sandhill Crane Festival** in November, where they journey from as far as Siberia. Free admission into exhibit halls and art shows. The festival's nature tours are fascinating and vary in cost.

615   Challenge the kids to a game of **giant jenga** at New Republic bar and grill.

616   Grab a stick and play a season of **field hockey** for the Sacramento Black Sticks (ages 12 & up), or just watch a high school or college field hockey game.

617   Pack up some blankets and pillows for **Free Movie Nights in Sacramento Parks**. Check *SactownMag. com* for their annual round-up late May or early June.

618   Try some new varieties of sweet tomatoes at the
       annual **Tomato Taste-Off** at Sunrise Mall Farmer's
       Market in August.

619   Get up close with the **Sacramento Philharmonic
       and Opera** at a free family concert with the Cre8tive
       Concerts program. Past free concerts have been in
       the summer months at local parks. A great way to see
       professional concert musicians.

620   Rent a **practice hole** at Mather Golf Course, dump
       out a bucket, and have a ball. Luscious scenery, happy
       kids.

621   Explore a nature trail around **Folsom Lake** in
       the springtime, and enjoy a variety of **colorful
       wildflowers**, including California poppy, Indian
       paintbrush, larkspur, lupine, fiddleneck, bordicaea,
       Dutchmen's pipe, and monkey flower.

622   **Become trained in astrophotography** together.
       Take a nighttime photography class through REI
       with a parent and go out to take pictures of the
       best starscapes in the area and learn techniques of
       shooting in limited light using exposure bracketing
       and a tripod. Recommended for teens, 4 hours. $39
       members, $44 non-members.

623   **Hear the retelling of your favorite childhood tales** at the **Sacramento Storybook Festival** by the Del Paso Blvd Partnership in October, and immerse yourself in the wonderful imaginative world of books. *dpbpartnership.com*

624   Visit five different types of **tarantula spiders** in the red barn at Fairytale Town.

625   Take in some waterfalls with the older kids. Hike the relatively easy 2.1-mile **Black Holes of Calcutta Falls** hike during spring when the waterfalls are at their peak water levels. By late summer they are usually dried up.

626   **Get permission to look at the sun.** On the first Saturday of the month, go to the safe solar viewings at the Community Observatory at Folsom Lake College. Always check online calendar before going, cancellations due to weather are made at least 60 minutes ahead of scheduled events.

627   Wear green and gold and cheer on **Sac State's Hornets (Division I)** Hornets in gymnastics, soccer, basketball, football, volleyball, and track.

628   Find out if you can get out of the escape room within 60 minutes, at **Escape Sacramento** on I St. Recommended for ages 10 & up. Kids of all ages are allowed only if the family books the whole room.

629 **Launch a boat** into the American River at Discovery Park.

630 Pick out some fresh, local flowers for someone you love at **Midtown Farmers Market** on J St. on Saturday morning, visit the kids zone, get some lemonade, and marvel at all the beautiful, colorful fruit our farmers are growing.

631 Get inspired by color and form at the family-friendly **Art Receptions at Blue Line Arts** every 3rd Saturday of the month 5:30-8:30pm in Roseville.

632 Get a detailed **tree tour and map** of the following Sacramento parks: Capitol Park, Southside Park, Gibbons Park, Woodlake Park, River Park, McKinley Park, Del Campo Park, American River College, Arden Park and Sacramento State Quad. Bring a picnic and let kids spend time feeling the leaves and bark of each tree and making observations. Download tree maps at: *sactree.com/treetours*

633 Lego addicts beware, you'll never be able to get the kids out of **Lego Bricks Fest**, where they can play mini golf on a Lego course, see intricate glow-in-the-dark creations, race their own derby car creations down a 35-foot long track, and build gigantic, life-sized buildings. Over a million Lego bricks are available to build anything you can imagine.

634   Pan for **shiny flecks of gold** in the American River, in the exact same spot where the gold rush was started in 1848, when James W. Marshall found gold in a puddle on the South Fork of the American River – in the valley the Nisenan Indians knew as "Cullumah." Marshall Gold Discovery State Historic Park, Coloma, CA. Hit up Argonaut Farm to Fork Cafe for a healthy lunch or Squally's On the River for some pizza with river views.

635   Take the **Urban Adventure Quest** for San Francisco (they have one for Sacramento too) and work as a team to figure out clues and puzzles, learning facts and history, visiting interesting places covering a couple of miles.

636   Who doesn't love a tiny house on wheels? Get your fix at **The Real RV Show**, with hundreds of the newest RV's on display at Cal Expo twice a year, during spring and fall. Free for kids under 12.

637   Carve, sculpt, and explore the basics of photography at a **kid-friendly mini studio camp at Verge Center for the Arts** during Sac Open Studios in September.

638   Visit the small parcel of land that was first purchased for the American River Parkway, the **S.A.R.A. Access**, which stands for Save the American River Association. See what the naturalists and preservationists envisioned, and keep an eye out for jack rabbits and deer. Nearby Waterton Access point is just down the block.

639   Take the whole family to play some outdoor lawn games at a self-described **family-friendly and dog-friendly vineyards in nearby Lodi**: Durst Winery & Estate, Harmony Wynelands, Jessie's Grove Winery, Klinker Brick Winery, LangeTwins Winery & Vineyards, Lodi Vintners, Macchia, McCay Cellars, Mettler Family Vineyards, Michael David Winery, Ripken Vineyards & Winery, Viaggio Estate & Winery, or Woodbridge by Robert Mondavi. Tip: You may have to request the lawn games from the front desk, but each winery has stated they are available. Plus, wine tastings are typically just $5 in Lodi, free if you buy a bottle. Don't forget to pack a picnic! Find a full listing of Lodi wineries and all their different amenities at *lodiwine.com*

640   Look for beavers and muskrat in the **Mormon Island Wetlands** in Folsom.

641   Take a **thrilling helicopter tour** of Sacramento and the Sierra Foothills with a local company like Cloud 9 Living or Capitol Helicopters. Be forewarned, it's not cheap.

642   Transport to Germany at **Turn Verein's Oktoberfest** or Maifest (in May) and enjoy maypole dancing, German games, crafts, and treats.

643   Make a real wood project at **Lowe's Build & Grow Clinic** for kids Saturdays at 10am. Pre-register at *lowesbuildandgrow.com*

644   Pack a picnic and take a dip **Kiva Beach** at South Lake Tahoe, where the water is warmer and shallower than most of the lake because it sits on a high shelf. Perfect for paddle boarding or floating out on an inner tube with the little ones. Enjoy the stunning views of Mount Tallac and the Sierra Nevadas.

645   Kick back on an inner tube and **float down the lazy river** at Raging Waters at Cal Expo. Mini slides for toddlers and thrilling slides for older kids make this a magnet for kids in the summertime.

646   **Wakeboard, water ski, kneeboard** on Lake Natoma at the Waterski Family Night at the Sacramento State Aquatic Center.

647   Take a **walk at dusk** in your Sacramento
      neighborhood and listen for sounds you don't notice
      during daylight. Our hearing senses peak when
      there are less visuals. Wear a headlamp for an extra
      dimension of fun. Look for worms hanging out in the
      grass, but don't bother them. They're essential for
      soil health.

648   There's Japanese karate, and then there's a different
      Korean and Chinese style called **Tang Soo Do
      karate**, which you can take up at Genevieve Didion
      Elementary School in the Pocket neighborhood with
      the City of Sacramento recreation program. Ages
      7-13. Physically-challenged kids encouraged.

649   Tailgate at the **West Wind Drive-In Movie Theaters**
      and see a family-friendly flick. Bring popcorn and
      blankets and snuggle up! Tuesdays are family fun
      nights, adults are $5.25. Kids are always $1.25.

650   Download the app **OldSacramento** to get the
      backstory on historic monuments in Old Sac, take the
      self-guided tour, and play games.

651   Try some rolled ice cream with toppings at **Ice Panda**
      in Elk Grove.

652   See the next, hilarious family-friendly musical by the **River City Theatre Company** in the Hiram Johnson High School Auditorium. Take part in their next kids theatre workshop, held twice a year, and maybe even audition for their next production.

653   Inspire environmental activism in kids at the annual **Wild & Scenic Film Festival** in Nevada City and Grass Valley in January. Includes kids activities, live music, and workshops.

654   Take a break from the books, and play some **ABCmouse educational games** on computers at the Sacramento Public Library.

655   Climb aboard the **Delta King**, an authentic 285-foot steamboat that was built in Glasgow, Scotland, and ferried passengers to and from San Francisco between 1927-1940. It used to take 10.5 hours. Make it an occasion and share a Brioche French Toast or Gluten Free Pancakes at the Pilothouse restaurant (on the boat) with some of the best river views.

656   Get some hot cocoa at Old Soul Weatherstone on 21st and walk to the **100-year old (allegedly) haunted mansion** that looks like it could be home to the Addams Family, complete with gargoyles and ornate wooden balconies. This is a private residence, please be respectful, 2131 H Street (corner of 22nd).

657 Use **Adobe Creative Suite** (Photoshop, InDesign, Lightroom, etc.) at the Design Spot at Arcade Public Library to make some interesting designs to your favorite photo or make a collage. **Print your creation out on the special, large format printer** (13" x 19") and hang it in your home.

658 Laugh your way through the **Nutty Nutcracker**, Sacramento Ballet's kid-friendly homage to the holiday classic.

659 Go swimming at **Manor Pool** at Slide Hill Park in Davis, where the diving board, water slide, wading pool, and splash pad will keep the kids busy for hours.

660 **Calling all kidpreneurs** with big ideas! Develop a brand, create a product or service, build a marketing strategy, and open for business at the one-day marketplace, Acton Children's Business Fair in December.

661 **Donate your old bike** to the Sacramento Sheriff's Toy Project, and give it to a child in need.

662 Animals and storytime in a bakery? Yep, head on down to **Karen's Bakery in Old Folsom** every second Tuesday of the month for a book reading and visit by a special animal from the Folsom Zoo.

663   Rent a canoe for the **afternoon at Donner Lake**. Stock up on healthy lunch wraps, sandwiches, fresh-squeezed juices, and abundant fruit at New Moon Natural Foods on Donner Pass Road in Truckee.

664   **Paint the dreamy roses** at McKinley Park rose garden with watercolor or pastels.

665   Take an underground tour with **Old Sacramento Underground** in Old Sac, and see how the city literally lifted itself up during floods in the 1800s. Tours run April through December, recommended for kids ages 6 & up, 5 & under are free.

666   Venture to South Natomas Community Park for **Natomas Pops in the Park** for festive music, Sacto Mofo food trucks, bounce houses, a beer and wine garden, and free bike parking.

667   Take your bike for a DIY tune-up at the **Dero Fixit bike repair station** at the Arcade Public Library.

668   Go to the **Annual Electricity Fair** by the river at the Folsom Powerhouse State Historic Park in September, and learn about how sunlight and water can generate power. Fun kids activities include scavenger hunts, touring the powerhouse, seeing electric cars, and building series and parallel circuits.

669   Go to the fun and festive **Christmas Tree Lighting in Folsom** on Historic Sutter Street. Activities include carolers, train rides, live music, and a visit from Santa.

670   Get a stopwatch and try to **beat your own record** at sprinting. Improve your time at a regulation track, like on a local high school track. Start with a short distance.

671   Design and **create a 3D object** at TinkerCAD.com (or alter an existing design) and then take it down to print at **Sacramento Public Library's Makerspace** (Central branch) or **Tom Sanderson Design Spot** (Arcade branch). They currently have 3 Makerbot Replicator 2 machines, 1 Makerbot Replicator 5th Generation, 1 PrintrBot Jr. You can e-mail make@ saclibrary.org to make an appointment at the Central location during the weekday. One 3D print per person per day. They also offer 3D design classes for beginners. *saclibrary.org*

672   Get some bricks and mortar from a local Sacramento hardware store, like Ace Hardware, and **build a backyard fire pit** for spontaneous s'mores nights.

673   Do some candle dipping and gourd painting at
the very unique and crafty **Harvest Faire at the
Sacramento Waldorf School in Fair Oaks** every
year in October. They've been hosting it every
year for 45 years, and feature live music, handcrafted goods,
artisan foods and... zip-lining! Free.

674   Spend a second Thursday night May through October
at **Gather: Oak Park** with outdoor interactive art,
live music, artisanal food vendors, designers, and
a modular kids park. Food truck dining gets a fancy
upgrade with the super-long, white linen-covered
dining table on 3rd Ave.

675   Print out a **birdwatching** checklist from the
Sacramento Audubon Society's website, take a nature
walk with binoculars, and see how many different
birds you can identify.

676   Thespians wanted! Enroll in the low-cost
DramaMatters Afterschool drama education
program at the Boys and Girls Club Sacramento. Ages
6-18.

677   Hit up the mall for a **themed photo op**. Visit the
Easter Bunny or Santa and his helpers for a cute (or
funny) photo op at Arden Fair Mall, Roseville Mall,
Sunrise Mall, and others.

678 Rent the **Reverse Charades game** or Fluxx (the ever-changing card game for older kids) at the Arcade Public Library's "Library of Things," invite a friend over, and get ready for some weeknight fun.

679 Catch the early bird $3 bowling on weekend mornings 9-12pm at **Strikes Unlimited**, a high-tech, 50-lane bowling alley in Rocklin.

680 Play simple baseball games like **home run derby or ghost runner** at your nearest Sacramento city park baseball field.

681 Take the next free **"Birding for Families"** walk at the Effie Yeaw Nature Center, especially in the cool fall weather. Some of the nature trail is stroller-friendly.

682 Become experienced outdoors and gain real, valuable skills in the **Boy Scouts or Cub Scouts** with the Golden Empire Council (Sacramento's regional Boy Scouts group). Activities include hiking, camping, mountain biking, kayaking, and more, with an emphasis on social responsibility and volunteering. Girls can join now too.

683 Make some hot holiday drinks in a thermos and set out to walk (or wheel) around the **decked-out "Fab 40's" in East Sacramento at Christmas**. Start at 42nd St. between Folsom Blvd. and J Street.

684   Get a few neighborhood kids together and **play some softball at Doc Oliver Field** in William Land Park, Playfields Park in Davis, or your nearest softball diamond (Grant Park, Northgate Park, O'Neil Field, Redwood Park, Reichmuth park, Roosevelt Park, Tahoe Park).

685   Rent a **Yamaha Portable Keyboard** from Sacramento Public Library's "Library of Things" and learn by heart a simple and easy duet, like "Heart & Soul."

686   Kick of festival season in May with **First Festival**, a celebration of music with modern art installations, food, craft beer, face painting, and more.

687   Find a **free little library** in your Sacramento neighborhood at *freelittlelibrary.org*. If none exists, build one.

688   Dance the night away at a **father-daughter dance**, like the annual Father Daughter Dance in Fair Oaks at the Community Clubhouse (*fairoakspark. org*), the Daddy & Me Valentines Dance in Eldorado Hills (*eldoradohillsCSD.org*), or with Fancy Feet (*fancyfeetdance.net*).

689   **Shadow veterinarians** and discover the world of animal science at the youth programs at the Sacramento SPCA.

690 **Specialize in rowing** with the River City Rowing
Club youth programs (ages 10 & up) or a rowing camp
with Capital Crew at Sacramento State Aquatic Center
(ages 12 & up).

691 Cool off on a hot summer afternoon at Morse Park
splash pad in Elk Grove.

692 Grab a box of local **California kumquats** in winter
and delight in eating them whole – their skins are
edible! They are like teeny, tiny oranges you can eat
in one bite. Keep an eye out for them at the farmer's
market November-March or call the Sacramento
Natural Foods Co-op, Sprouts, Raley's, or Whole
Foods to check if they are in-stock.

693 **Rent a raft and float down the river**, and catch
a shuttle back to your car (every 30 minutes on
weekends) with River Rat in Fair Oaks.

694 See the natural world through the eyes of scientists on a free **"Critter Walk"** public tour of the Mather Field vernal pools by Sacramento Splash in March. Register early, as these events sell out.

695 Hear a variety of rock, reggae, latin, country, blues, and jazz at the free, family-friendly **Summer Concert Series at the Palladio at Broadstone** in Folsom on Wednesday nights. It moves to the Historic District Amphitheater on Thursdays, and Folsom City Lions Park on Fridays.

696 Sign-up for **Kids in the Kitchen** at **Pizza Rock** and make your very own pizza with your own two hands. It's held the first Saturday of each month, $11 per child, starts at 11am. All proceeds go to charity.

697 Continue Martin Luther King's Jr.'s dream for a better world by walking in the free **MLK365's March For The Dream** in January. The march starts at Sacramento City College and ends at the Sacramento Convention Center, where a Diversity Expo features books, robotics demonstrations, green tech cars, radio stations, health screenings, and more. If that's too far for the kids, join in at any point on the route, even the last 3 blocks, and enjoy the Expo.

698 Play a family game of **shuffle board** at Top Golf in Roseville.

699 Watch some **modern ballet** or contemporary dance at the Mondavi Center in Davis.

700 **Help Monarch butterflies thrive** in the Sacramento Valley. Visit the National Wildlife Federation's website after March for a free summer butterfly gardening kit when you take the Butterfly Heroes pledge.

701 See relics of the pioneer days, family stories, and a **real family carriage** from the 1800s at the quaint, historic Carnegie Museum in Roseville, which was originally built as the first public library in Roseville. Don't miss the toy train exhibit modeled after the town of Roseville. Hours are limited, as with all small museums, but off-hours tours can be scheduled for just $20, for groups of ten or less. Free.

702 **Fly a kite on a windy day** in an open field like Granite Regional Park in Sacramento or Playfields Park in Davis.

703 Go to a **free, world-class concert** by renown international musicians passing through the new **Ann E. Pitzer Center** at UC Davis.

704 Go wakeboarding, if you're over 42" inches, at **Velocity Island Park** in Woodland.

705 Boogie down at **Fair Oak's free Concerts in the Park** every Thursday in the summer at Village Park.

706   Take a **45-minute summer train ride** along the
       Sacramento River, starting at the California Railroad
       Museum. Free for ages 5 & under.

707   Get a creative and delicious **shaved snow treat** at
       Vampire Penguin on K Street.

708   Ride a little red wagon to a **construction site** in
       downtown Sacramento (or closer to your house), and
       try identify each machine and vehicle. Ask questions.
       The workers are usually glad to explain what's going
       on.

709   Drop-in at the **Lakeshore Learning** store in Roseville
       on a Saturday 11am-3pm for a free colorful craft
       activity. Ages 3 & up.

710   Dance your way down to the **One Love One Heart
       Reggae Festival** in September. No one's too young to
       soak up Bob Marley's music.

711   Explore deeply carved **petroglyphs at night** by
       lantern at the next Rock Art Mysteries tour at the
       Maidu Museum & Historic Site in Roseville.

712   Grab a flashlight and go on a spooky **lantern tour
       of the Sacramento Historic City Cemetery** in
       October. The cemetery's lush and ornate beauty will
       surprise you.

713   **Get ready for your first job.** Roll up your sleeves, write up a resume, and go down to the **Youth Job & Resource Fair** at City Hall in April to find out about the myriad of volunteer, internship, and job opportunities in Sacramento. Recommended for 16 & up, but the fair encourages younger kids to attend for volunteer opportunities.

714   Watch the **Harlem Globetrotters** perform a funny, exciting show full of incredible spinning, dribbling, acrobatics, and daring hoop shots in January at the Golden1 Center. Fun music and audience participation makes this show an enduring annual tradition. Go to their website beforehand and learn all of their nutty stage names, like Crazy Joe, Spider, Animal, Ant, Hi-Lite, and Big Easy.

715   Get a bite to eat at the beautiful and modern **Barnes & Nobles in Folsom at the Palladio** and stay for storytime on Saturdays. Wine bar and beer on tap available.

716   Go see the eccentric **"Dragon House"** in Curtis Park, a private home with fantastical mosaic ceramic art on the side, depicting a two-story, fire-breathing dragon, fairies, owls, and more. Created by a local art teacher in the mid-1980s. 2816 22nd St., Sacramento. Please be respectful, as this is a private residence.

717   Take a **free 45-minute introductory ballroom dancing lesson** at Malko Dance Academy, whose junior team recently won the US National Junior Smooth Ballroom Competition. Ages 4-16.

718   Hit the gas at the **Stockholm Raceway** and challenge each other at some outdoor kart racing at Scandia Fun Center. Must be 54" to drive, 36" to ride.

719   See some ridiculously well-dressed pets at the **Flower Farm's Annual Pet Parade** in October.

720   Have a **family foosball challenge** at John's Incredible Pizza in Roseville. Enjoy the unlimited salad bar.

721   Ride the only **water roller coaster** in California at Golfland SunSplash, coasting at 40 miles per hour, down 5 stories. Must be 42" to ride with an adult.

722   Find out when Myrtle Press is having their next free **Printmaking Demo** and watch the art of printing come alive.

723   Share a bowl of **Italian gelato** at a local gelateria, like Devine's, Miabella, Eatuscany, or our hands-down favorite **Conscious Creamery**, a plant-based gelato-maker. They don't have a shop yet but they serve up delectable scoops at various events in Sacramento and San Francisco. Check their pop-up calendar at: *https://www.consciouscreamery.com/calendar/*

724   Hit up the free **R Street Block Party** when the
       weather's nice in May for the newest handmade goods
       made by local makers, plus a kids zone, live music,
       local food.

725   Join other Lego enthusiasts at Sacramento Public
       Library's kid-friendly **Lego Block Party** or Lego
       Mania events.

726   See some breathtaking pottery by the Sacramento
       Potters Group, at their annual **Art by Fire Holiday
       Show** in the Fall.

727   Teach kids how to keep plastic and packaging from
       filling up the landfills. Take a trip to **Refill Madness**
       on 29th St. and refill your own bottles from home with
       more than 300 eco-friendly products, with everything
       from shampoos to laundry detergent.

728   Take a **puppet-making class or workshop**. Fairytale
       Town hosts puppet-making camps every summer.
       Make your own at home and put on a little skit for a
       family member.

729   Test your strength and balance on the Double Trouble
       obstacle course at **Wackford Aquatic Complex** in
       Elk Grove. Three fun pools come with a water slide
       and high and low diving board. Little ones can enjoy
       the wading pool and water features. Under 2 free, 2-4
       $3, 5 & older $6. Double Trouble wristband $2.

730   If you're in passing Vacaville, take a stroll through the Consolidated Rock & Mineral Shop, or simply **"Rock Shop"** as it reads on the barn-like building facing Highway 80. They have an enormous collection of stones and fossils, crystals and gems, in every color of the rainbow. Don't miss the fossilized fish and the giant amethyst clusters. Be sure to label anything you buy, so you can read up on it later. 5115 Quinn Rd, Vacaville.

731   Every second Saturday in summer, cut up some watermelon and shimmy over to East Sacramento's **Pops in the Park** to listen to live music by a wide variety of local acts. Park sites vary. Ride bikes or get there early to get good parking and set up your blanket or lawn chairs.

732   Dance among 300,000 daffodils (300 varieties) at **Daffodil Hill** in Amador County. This flower farm has been lovingly cared for by the McLaughlin family since 1887. Open only during daffodil season, around late-March to mid-April. Call for exact dates and times.

733   Take part in a Run, Jump, Throw Camp in February with the **Revolution Express Track Club**, and take your athletic goals to the next level. Ages 7-14.

734   Celebrate all things Western at the annual **Elk Grove Western Festival** in May at Elk Grove Regional Park.

735   Take the whole family for some **old-school roller skating** fun at Foothill Skate Inn on Wednesday Family Night.

736   Visit **Busy Kidz** in Folsom for some toddler fun in a miniature city modeled after historic Sutter Street in Folsom. Snuggle up in the reading bungalow. $1 Coffee and Tea every Thursday.

737   Hear what a **"guitar orchestra"** sounds like at the Sacramento Guitar Society's performance in December.

738   Go to a **free family concert and instrument petting zoo** by the wonderful **Camellia Symphony Orchestra** at Central Public Library, usually in early December.

739   Be adventurous and **try some Afghan food and desserts** at Bamiyan Afghan Restaurant in El Dorado Hills or Chopan Kabob House in Elk Grove.

740   Take a sailing summer camp at Sacramento State Aquatic Center and learn **how to sail** your own sailboat in one week. Ages 12 & up.

741   **Create your own National Day** for something (big or small) you believe in. A month before your day, send a press release to the Sac Bee, SNR, and NPR with the story behind your idea.

742   See the works of local and Bay Area dance companies at the annual **Sacramento State Dance Sampler** showcase, usually in April. *csus.edu/dram*

743   Go to a rose garden (like McKinley Park or the State Capitol) and do a **color scavenger hunt**. Create a checklist of every color the rainbow (except black) and see who can check off all the colors first.

744   Your enchanting lake front room with a view is waiting at **Sly Park Recreation Area's** campgrounds. Reserve a site, grab a tent, fixin's for food, and go!

745   Learn how to **pickle peaches** (or just eat fresh ones) at **Sacramento's Peach Festival** in Carmichael in August. California is the top producer of peaches in the world. Older kids can go head-to-head with adults in the pie-eating contest.

746 Try a Hong Kong-style **rolled ice cream** at Sixteen Degrees Fahrenheit on Stockton Blvd. It's like ice cream, but in chewy roll-ups with toppings. Or, if you're closer to Land Park, hit up **8 Fahrenheit.**

747 **Listen to some choir music**, especially at Christmas time, at Bethany Presbyterian Church on 24th St. Check *sacchoralcalendar.com* for free events.

748 Kids under 12 can **munch on a free basket of fruit** at the front of the produce section at **Raley's** grocery stores, as part of their Let's Begin nutrition program to promote healthy eating and overall wellness for children.

749 **Play a board game** on a cozy blanket under a tree in autumn at the Capitol State Park. There's usually more available street parking on the south side of the park, rather than the north.

750 Eat at a restaurant totally staffed by culinary students. **The Oak Café** at American River College will inspire future foodies with their meticulously plated, seasonal, artistic dishes. Older kids can chat with staff about their culinary education. And for the littles, there's usually a delicious pizza option and inventive desserts. Explain to the kids that the servers are training to become chefs.

751   **Spend $10 on a new-for-you outfit** at Thrift
Town. Get a $5 off coupon (on a $15 purchase) in the
Sacramento News & Review weekly.

752   For toddlers who want some **mini trees to explore
and climb**, look not further than the dozen or so
camellia trees just a few yards east of the McKinley
Park Rose Garden.

753   **Design a box of chocolates at Ginger Elizabeth
Chocolates** in midtown, or go to their next monthly
ice cream socials on summer Saturdays starting
at 10am and split a sundae ($9) made from locally
sourced ingredients at their peak. Dates vary, check
their schedule.

754   **Eat pizza for breakfast** on Sundays at Scoreboards
Pizza & Grill in Roseville. Veggie options available.

755   Pick up some **Hong Kong-style coconut buns**,
crepes, or sponge rolls at Pegasus Bakery & Cafe.

756   Get the kids in to the **Sacramento Zoo for free** with
a paying adult on Wells Fargo Wednesdays, the first
Wednesday of the month.

757   **See the inner workings of a news station**, and
maybe inside the set of Good Day Sacramento.
CBS Sacramento is one of the only TV stations in
Sacramento to offer family or group tours. Call their
community manager to set-up a tour.

758   Pick out a truly one-of-a-kind, quality birthday gift for a friend at **Koukla Kids**, a quirky kids' boutique in East Sacramento. Wander around the corner of the building and enter the eccentric **Geographica** shop, where owner Mark Anderson curates rare maps, globes, and other interesting artifacts from across the globe.

759   Play with **modern kids toys and furniture** in the kids section of **IKEA.** Eye-rolls, perhaps, but with 99-cent breakfast and free coffee for IKEA family members, it deserves a mention. Let little ones play in Småland (free supervised play area) while you shop.

760   Take up a cause that affects you and your family and participate in a **political march to the Capitol**.

761   Roam through the peach orchard at certified organic **Sun Smile Farms** in Grass Valley and pick your own to take home. Must arrange with them beforehand what you want to pick and they will set-up a time. Peaches are usually ready Late June through September. They also have cherries, blackberries, raspberries, and flowers available for u-pick (also by appointment only).

762   **See what planets are visible** in tonight's night sky. It can be exhilarating to find planets to look at. *timeanddate.com/astronomy/night/usa/sacramento*

763   Explore painting, clay, and glazed ceramics at the kid-friendly open studio at **Art Bistro** in Rocklin, with good food and wine. $10 painting special on Tuesdays. Ages 6 & up.

764   Slurp up some **"bubble tea"** tapioca balls through extra-large straws at **Quickly** on 16th St. Instead of tea, kids can order from the long menu of slushy drinks and still order it with the sweet, chewy tapioca balls.

765   Go to the next **Warehouse Book Sale** at the Friends of the Sacramento Public Library's Book Den for gently used children's books at the lowest prices.

766   Ride the **kiddie train at the Fountains in Roseville**. Tickets are available at the kiosk next to the fountain at the center of the outdoor mall. $2 per ride.

767   Ride your bike to the **U.S. Bicycling Hall of Fame** in Davis and catch a glimpse of champions from the 1880's to the present and learn about all aspects of biking, including road, track, motocross, BMX, mountain biking, and cyclocross. Open Wednesdays 4-6pm and Saturdays 10am-2pm.

768 Beyond the rides and live music, the **California State Fair** boasts impressive educational and interactive exhibits for kids of all ages on food, agriculture, science, technology, arts, and crafts. Scan the schedule in July for children's authors, photography exhibits, or anything else that catches your interest.

769 Meet children's book authors, play in the kids zone, stay for a poetry reading, and watch the community parade at the **Sacramento Black Book Fair** in June.

770 Go to **Goodwill** or REI and put together an **adventure backpack**: good binoculars, bird/duck call, compass, flashlight, magnifying glass, etc. Get more ideas at *sactownkids.com/adventurebackpack*

771 Bump around and spray each other with water at **Baltic Sea Bumper Boats** at Scandia Fun Center. Must be 44" to drive, 40" to ride.

772 Take the mine tour at **Hangtown Gold Bug Park**. Huddle through the chilly cavernous corridors and imagine the strenuous life of a miner and what they looked for in the rock. Watch a volunteer blacksmith hammer and mold something right before your eyes.

773 Roller skate all night at **Roller King Roseville on Family Night**, $17 for 5 skaters.

774 Take a **youth archery class** at Wilderness Archery in Rocklin. Ages 7-16, equipment included.

775   Go to **storytime in an art gallery** at Verge Center for the Arts, in conjunction with Sacramento Public Library. They currently do storytimes there every couple of months, when there's a new exhibit.

776   **Experience Hmong culture** and celebrate the Hmong New Year at Cal Expo in November.

777   **Rent a paddle board** from SUP South Lake Tahoe, and they'll supply your car with the racks to carry the board so that you can take it anywhere you want. You can **paddle to nearby Emerald Bay** from Baldwin Beach.

778   Visit the indoor showroom at **Kidz Backyard** in Rancho Cordova to see a dizzying array of wooden backyard playsets, spring-free trampolines, basketball hoops, and more.

779   Dance to live music in the summer at **First Friday Street Fair** and **Saturday Night Concerts** at Fountains at Roseville. Face-painting and lots of family-friendly fun.

780   Take little, budding gardeners on a daytrip to Santa Rosa for the **National Heirloom Exposition** in Santa Rosa. The "world's fair of pure food" is the largest display of heirloom produce in the country, with unique and funky varieties on display.

781   **Stay in a cabin** next to the American River near Coloma, like American River Resort, Coloma Resort, or Camp Lotus. Go swimming, rafting, pan for gold, or do the ropes challenge course at Coloma Resort.

782   Train-loving kids will love grabbing lunch at **Pacific Street Café** in Roseville, with a viewing platform to watch real trains go by outside, plus a toy train that is on-the-go at all times inside the restaurant.

783   **Walk or bike to a downtown farmer's market** almost any day of the week: **Roosevelt Park** (9th & P St.) on Tuesdays May through September, **Chavez Plaza** (10th & J St.) on Wednesdays May through October, **Capitol Mall** (6th & Capitol Mall) on Thursdays May through September, **Midtown** (20th & J St.) on Saturdays all year-round, and **State Parking Lot** on Thursdays under the freeway (8th & W St.) all year-round.

784   Drop in for a **Sunday "Sketch It" session** at the Crocker Art Museum, and get casual drawing instruction while drawing at your own pace in one of the galleries. Free with admission, all ages, supplies provided.

785   Sign up for the next **free kids golf clinic** at Diamond Oaks Golf Course or Woodcreek Golf Club, usually in May. Kids can also play free with a paying adult during certain times of the year.

786   Go on a **rare plant treasure hunt at the Consumnes River Preserve**, and take pictures of all the funny-looking plants you've never seen before. Make a rare plant journal. Do this for strange insects and critters you encounter too.

787   Bring your favorite board game to the downtown Roseville public library every second Saturday for **"Board at the Library"** and make new friends.

788   Test out some **lesser-known instruments** at Kline music. Take a banjo, ukulele, or folk harp lesson.

789   **Roast some marshmallows** at your favorite park an hour before sunset, and dip them in some homemade hot chocolate. Bring a self-burning log and lighter, and find a picnic table next to a grill. Memorize a short campfire story to tell.

790   Expand your knowledge of **African American history** through art at the Sojourner Truth African Heritage Museum. Drop in for the First Saturdays Family Art Day from 12-2pm.

791   **Talk to the Canadian geese** at McKinley Park pond. Try to identify the ducks you see. Mallards are common nesters in the Sacramento Valley, as are wood ducks, gadwalls, and cinnamon teal. Between one and three million ducks, geese, and swans use the Sacramento Valley as a wintering ground.

792   Pick a truly unique, artful gift for the next children's birthday you attend at **Art of Toys** downtown, where artists make cool toys from art or make art from toys. Either way, the kids will have fun poking around the imaginative objects.

793   Board the **Spookamotive Train Ride** at California State Railroad Museum at the end of October, and learn about witches and wizards on decorated trains.

794   Take a **free Lil' Samurai or Teen martial arts class** at Kovar Satori's Academy of Martial Arts' nine locations in and near Sacramento.

795   **Get into a tree pose** and stretch out at free outdoor yoga in the park with **Yoga Moves Us** at various scheduled locations: McKinley Park, the River City Food Bank, Tahoe Park, Maidu Park in Roseville, Community Park in Davis, and Lions Park in Folsom. *yogamovesus.org*

796   Treat older kids to a **foot massage** at Happy Day Spa (if you need one too) for $25 for one hour, and then grab some Thai noodles at nearby Lollibowl.

797   **Go mountain biking** along Folsom Lake with a mountain biking expert and learn tricks on how to navigate minor obstacles on trails, riding techniques, and body/pedal position. Enroll at REI. Ages 14 & up.

798   Go to a **bilingual storytime** for Spanish stories and songs, at the North Highlands Public Library.

799   Go to a yarn shop, like **Rumplestiltskin** near the Capitol or Knitique in Elk Grove, and learn how to knit the simplest socks.

800   Go on kiddie roller coaster or mini airplane ride at **Funderland** in Land Park.

801   Celebrate Earth Day in April with **Roseville's Earth Festival** with everything from live music, fashion shows, science experiments, free face painting, bee shows, Roseville PD's K-9 demonstrations. Free bike parking, food trucks, and an earth-friendly scavenger hunt are just a few reasons to go.

802   Watch the **Statehood Celebratory Procession** on Labor Day, complete with a brass band, Living History characters, donkeys, horses, wagons, and wacky street performers.

803   Travel back in time and watch shoes being meticulously and lovingly handmade by **Benjamins** shoemakers at the WAL studios on R St. They usually have someone available to chat and answer questions about shoemaking. Grab a fresh-pressed juice in the food court on your way out.

804 **Skip rocks at a cozy, picturesque beach** with public access like Sarah Court along the American River Parkway. It's nestled between two private homes and includes a parking lot. Bring a picnic.

805 **See what a City Council meetings looks like**, every Tuesday 5pm at City Hall, 915 I St. Make a public comment about something you care about at the end. For another activity while you're there, test all the batteries lying around the house beforehand, and take all the old ones to the battery drop-off at City Hall. Teach kids why batteries are toxic for the environment and banned from the landfills.

806 **Play checkers** or chess under a tree at a shady park like William Land Park. Play two out of three games, and the winner plays the next person.

807 Go for an easy camping weekend at the nearby **Peninsula Campground** on Folsom Lake, where 100 camp spots are situated near the water with fire rings, flush toilets, and showers.

808 **Become well-versed in making an emergency shelter**, how to access drinking water, and make an emergency kit at home at the Wilderness Survival 3-Season Skills class at REI. Ages 13 & up.

809 Simmer your favorite vegetables and rice noodles in **your own personal shabu pot** at a shabu restaurant like Heat Shabu Baru or Shabu Japanese Fondue.

810 **Tour a fire station** and climb aboard a real fire truck with the Sacramento Fire Department's Open House Program. Usually runs May through October on Saturday afternoons 2-4pm, free. Check the current schedule at: *cityofsacramento.org*

811 See a movie at a Sacramento park with summertime's **Screen On The Green**. Ride over on bikes and plop down for a family-friendly flick under the stars. Free popcorn – what?! Yes.

812 Go on a free Wildlife Observation **Paddle Tour** during summer at **Stone Lakes National Wildlife Refuge**.

813 Go to a **Sacramento Brick Builders Lego** meeting and learn cool techniques from veteran brick builders and hobbyists.

814 **Hike to Big Meadow** near Lake Tahoe, where wildflowers grow rampant in the spring. Continue on the trail with older kids to Round Lake, with incredible views of a rocky bluff and waterfall, about 3 miles in.

815 Munch on some **sweet Austrian bread** at Konditorei in Davis. The vanilla chocolate bread and strawberry bread are crowd-pleasers.

816 Soccer season over too soon? Join an **indoor youth soccer league** at Let's Play Indoor Soccer Arena, and play through winter.

817 For a budget-conscious, **introductory classical music concert** (for older kids), find out when the next Sacramento State Faculty & Ensemble concert is taking place. The faculty is quite accomplished and some have performed with the San Francisco Symphony and have worked on recordings for Broadway shows. They have soloists, as well as ensembles for wind instruments, strings, chamber, jazz, latin jazz, and more. $10 adults, $7 students.

818 Go **gem mining** and run through nature trails during the fall months at Apple Ridge Farms.

819 **Pick your own certified organic strawberries**, blackberries, and cherries at Goodness Orchard in the early summer. Reservations required.

820   Take the **Sacramento RiverTrain** for a 90-minute train ride that boards in West Sacramento on Harbor Blvd.

821   Spend the morning with black bears, red foxes, wolves, and coyotes at **Folsom Zoo Sanctuary**.

822   Twist up some **pad thai noodles** and try some mango sweet sticky rice, a famous Thai dessert, at any local Thai cafe like Thai Basil or Coconut on T. Coconut ice cream is also a sure-fire hit with kids.

823   Collect leaves in Land Park and make **colorful leaf rubbings** with paper and crayons. Try to identify the trees as they correspond to each leaf.

824   Customize your own personal pizza at **Pieology**, including four different doughs, five sauces, six cheeses (including vegan), and fourteen toppings. $8.79. Sacramento, Roseville, and Folsom.

825   Explore **Lake Natoma's hidden spots** with a kayaking class with Current Adventures. Classes run August through October. Kids are welcome with an adult.

826   Show your dog (or just adopt one) at the Sacramento Kennel Club's **AKC All-Breed Dog Show** in April. Free for 12 & under.

827   Get ready for some serious open spaces at Deer Creek
       Hills, with **4060-acres of rolling grasslands and
       blue oaks**. More than 170 species of birds will keep
       the binoculars warm.

828   Gear up for **train-themed storytime** every Monday
       at 11am at the California State Railroad Museum. Free
       with admission.

829   **Discover the process of treating wastewater**
       at a free, educational tour of the **Pleasant Grove
       Wastewater Treatment Plant**. After this behind-
       the-scenes look, kids will think twice about letting
       perfectly clean water go to waste while brushing their
       teeth or taking a shower. Ages 12 & up.

830   Go **indoor swimming in the wintertime** at
       Northern California **Swimstitute's** open family swim
       on Sundays 11:30-1:00pm in Rancho Cordova.

831   Go on an early morning 8am **bird walk with Soil
       Born Farm** guides around American River Ranch
       Park. $8. Winter and migrant birds abound in
       January.

832   Go **urban fishing** at Howe Park Pond or Southside
       Park Pond.

833 See thousands of **pharmacy artifacts**, as old as 200 years, at the **Don & June Salvatori Pharmacy Museum** in Natomas. By appointment only.

834 Build your own dreamland in the Lego sandbox at the next **BrickFest Live** Lego Fan Experience at the Sacramento Convention Center. Learn robotics, play Lego mini-golf, wander the glow zone, race some Lego cars, and see giant Lego exhibits that is the stuff of kids' dreams.

835 Organize a group of ten or more kids to deliver **Mugs with Hugs** to the elderly in Sacramento, many of whom never get visitors. Watch children's awareness and compassion grow. *mugswithhugs.com*

836 **Drop a fishing line** into the Sacramento River in Clarksburg. Grab a pole at Holland Market and ask them where to go.

837 Climb up some steep rocks and build your courage in a kids belay one-hour **rock climbing** session at Sacramento Pipeworks.

838 Plant a **butterfly garden** with marigold, zinnias, and dandelions to attract Sacramento Valley butterflies like the Monarch butterfly. Be sure to pick the Tagetes or Bidens variety of marigold, not the calendula (a.k.a. "Common Pot" or "English Marigold").

839 See if you can get through the **Marshall Splash Zone** inflatable obstacle course at the El Dorado Hills Community Pool... without falling off!

840 Go to a locally owned nursery, like Talini's on Folsom, and **pick an herb to grow indoors in the winter**. Place it next to a sunny window and use it often.

841 **Build a sand castle or float a handmade boat** made out of recycled materials at Sand Cove Beach. Attach it to a long string so it doesn't float away. Get ideas at *sactownkids.com/makeaboat*

842 Pick out some warm socks to donate to **Wind Youth Services**, a youth shelter in Sacramento. More than 400 minors and young people live on the streets of Sacramento. *windyouth.org*

843 Drop by the **Pokemon Club** at the Martha Riley Community Library in Roseville to trade cards, battle, and meet other Pokemon trainers. Second and fourth Saturdays, 2:30-4:30pm. Ages 5-13.

844 Make a family night of **badminton,** and serve up some birdies at the NorCal Badminton Club in Rancho Cordova. Take advantage of their family plans and first-timer $5 entry fee coupon on their website.

845 Check out the Capital City Yacht Club's **Holiday Lighted Boat Parade** in early December.

846   Skip rocks and do cartwheels at **Paradise Beach** just behind Glenn Hall Park. Play explorers and pirates and discover new land. Let the serene water rushing by lift your spirits and calm your mind.

847   Play **volleyball** on a real sand court, like at Swanston Park, Tahoe Park, or Walnut Park in Davis.

848   Play a **9-hole round of FlingGolf** on the Arcade Creek Golf Course at Haggin Oaks. FlingSticks rentals are included.

849   Take a free introductory private **ballroom dancing lesson** at Spotlight Ballroom in West Sacramento and do the foxtrot. They have youth programs for young dancers.

850   Find out how the **wind can turn on our light bulbs**, and how solar panels on your house can help climate change at the annual **Electricity Fair** at the Folsom Powerhouse State Historic Park in September. Families can tour the powerhouse, see electric vehicles up close, and take part in activities, exhibits, and prizes.

851   Learn how to **play chess with the whole family** at the Martin Luther King Jr. public library on select Saturdays.

852   During fall and spring semester, go to a **"Wonders of Astronomy"** presentation at Sierra College's Astronomy Department. Includes a slide show, a hands-on activity, and the projection of star images on the planetarium dome.

853   Find some Hachiya persimmons, and learn Hoshigaki, the **art of hand-dried persimmons**. It takes weeks and each persimmon must be squish and squeezed daily. Kids will love to help. Otow Orchard in Granite Bay is renown for keeping the tradition alive. *otoworchard.com/hoshigaki.html*

854   Try a real **French macaron** or a traditional, flaky, butter croissant at Estelle's Patisserie on Arden Way.

855   Experience **pioneer life** at the living history **McFarland Ranch** in Galt.

856   Pick up breakfast and **watch planes fly in and out of Sacramento International Airport** in the cell phone lot. For a better view of take-off, take the airport exit 258 off of I-5 (heading north), then take the south service road east for 1 mile, then turn left onto Powerline Road. There are a few places to pull off the road and watch the planes take flight. Follow all applicable road laws.

857 Hear kids of all ages play wind, string, and percussion instruments expertly and adeptly at a **Sacramento Youth Symphony** concert, usually free for ages 10 & under. Find out when their next open rehearsals are being held (usually in February) and get a fascinating insider's look into how a young symphony or orchestra practices.

858 **Study up on three magic tricks** to perform for your family while waiting for dinner to arrive in the caboose car at the Old Spaghetti Factory, or other old-timey restaurant.

859 **Pretend you're in Hawaii** at Lolo Island Hawaiian Shave Ice on Florin Road and get an Aloha Rainbow shaved ice or a non-dairy Pineapple Dole Whip soft serve, always a crowd-pleaser.

860 Find out when the next free **Family Karaoke Night** is taking place at the Sacramento Public Library.

861   Touch and feel Native basketry and crafts at the **All Nations Craft Fair** at the Maidu Activity Center (adjacent to the Maidu Museum) in December in Roseville. Meet more than 20 Native American artisans from California tribes and the Cherokee Nation. Watch tribal drumming, traditional music, and singing.

862   Take your dog to **Bannon Creek Dog Park** for some spontaneous fun and then explore the paths along the American River.

863   Pack an easy spaghetti or fruit picnic and play in the grass along the lake at **Nimbus Recreation Area**.

864   Sew a cat bed or dog bed or a simple, little blanket for the animals at **Front Street Animal Shelter**. Or call them and ask if they have any immediate needs for donations.

865   Take teens to the next Shakespeare play by **Big Idea Theatre** on Del Paso Blvd. They produce at least one Shakespeare per year in their season's line-up.

866   Find some calm energy and **take a kids yoga class together** at Sacramento Yoga Center, Yoga Shala Sacramento, or Kids Unplugged. Yoga and meditation decreases anxiety and depression in both adults and kids.

867   **Walk a tightrope** at one of these three designated
parks in Davis where slacklining is permitted: Oak
Grove, Covell Park and the Covell Greenbelt. Bring
your own gear and be sure to make it low to the
ground for little ones.

868   Take a "**how to ride a bike**" class at REI. It's never
too late to learn! Ages 5-11. Check for adult classes as
well.

869   Gain leadership skills, volunteer, and follow your
passions with the **Girl Scouts, Heart of Central
California.**

870   Be amazed by the energy of young, glittered-up
dancers and dance teams at the **Rainbow Regional
Dance Competition**, usually in April.

871   Watch your money grow with dividends. **Open up a
Youth Savings Account** at Golden 1 Credit Union.
All you need is $1 to start! Sacramento Credit Union
offers Youth Savings Share Account with a $30
deposit, and one-time $5 membership fee.

872   Join a low-cost intramural athletic league with the
Boys & Girls Club of Sacramento.

873   Pretend to hit some home runs at the **batting cages**
at Scandia Fun Center, where they have 8 fast pitch
cages and 7 slow pitch softball cages.

874   Get lost in two fun **corn mazes**, take toddlers on a quick 1/4-mile nature trail and lie down on the lawn with a picnic lunch at Delfino Farms, formerly Kids Inc.

875   Rent the portable Lightstream **movie projector** at the Arcade Public Library's "Library of Things", and stream your favorite movie on a white sheet background in your front yard.

876   Go bird watching, hiking, or **horse riding at Dry Creek Parkway**.

877   Swim year-round under a beautiful glass ceiling at the **Mike Shellito Indoor Pool** in Roseville. Recreational swim is Saturdays and Sundays 1-4pm.

878   Throw on some boots for the **Hoes Down Harvest Festival** at Full Belly Farm in October. National Geographic described the children's area as "the best in the state." You'll fall in love with this farm.

879   Get some **u-pick chestnuts** at Smokey Ridge Ranch. Say hi to the donkeys and sheep, and sit down for a farm-to-table lunch on their little beautiful pond.

880   Take a drive at dusk to see the Halloween festivities and unique décor in late October on **Venice Street in the Bridgeway** community in West Sacramento.

881   Get inspired by wildlife big and tiny on a tour of the **Yolo Bypass Wildlife Area**, October to June, on the mornings of every second Saturday.

882   Get up-close and personal with more than **100 antique tractors** at the **California Agriculture Museum**. In November and December they cover the tractors with holiday lights.

883   Catch some 50's vibes and play some sweet tunes on **old-fashioned jukeboxes** at Rick's Dessert Diner on J Street, while splitting a piece of their signature red velvet cake.

884   Get some top-notch **baseball and softball training** at a clinic or mini-camp taught by professional baseball players, college all-stars, and college coaches at **Extra Innings** in Rocklin.

885   Go to a weekend kid-friendly Storytime stage performance at **City Theatre at Sacramento City College**. Recent shows include Aesop's Fun Fables and Robin Hood in the Forest of Frogwarts. Opening day tickets are just $2.50.

886   Stop by Temple Coffee on K St. for some locally made desserts, with many vegan and gluten-free offerings, and **see a floor made out of 500,000 real copper pennies**.

887 Watch some of the **fastest cyclists in the world** race by the State Capitol in the annual Amgen Tour of California in May. Check the schedule to see when they hit Sacramento. It'll take your breath away.

888 Take a free **mountain biking tour** of Deer Creek Hills 4:30pm-dusk with the Sacramento Valley Conservancy and Folsom Auburn Trail Riders Action Coalition. Must pre-register online.

889 Don a headlamp and take a 50-minute walking tour of the **Black Chasm Cavern Caves**, a National Natural Landmark, about 60 miles away. Cave & Mine Adventures give walking tours and help you identify stalagmites, stalactites, and rare helictite crystals. Go gemstone mining right outside the visitor's center, which houses the large stalagmites that were used in Matrix trilogy. Buy a big geode ($10) to crack open with their very own, homemade geode-cracking tool. Walking tour, Adults $17.50, Kids ages 3-12 $9.50.

890 Visit Apple Hill in mid-to-late October for the **dramatic Arkansas Black apple** variety, a beautiful deep red-purple apple perfect for pies.

891 **Dance through wildflowers** and go on a nature-hike at the Sacramento Bar along the American River Parkway in springtime. Watch people salmon fishing in the winter.

892   Be enthralled by an epic movie on a super-gigantic screen at the **Esquire IMAX Theatre** on K Street.

893   Instead of letting your extra, overgrown fruits, vegetables, or herbs fall off and die, decorate some paper bags and make some **"harvest goody bags" for your favorite Sacramento friends and neighbors**. Building social communities makes for happier families.

894   **Experiment with Minecraft**, rocket cars, l egos, electronics, and crafts at Sacramento Public Library's STEAM (Science, Technology, Engineering, Arts, and Math) program afterschool events.

895   Test your quick wit and take a 2-hour youth workshop at **Comedy Spot** on J St. Ages 8 & up.

896   Shalom! Eat some latkes and bagels at the annual **Jewish Food Faire**, a family event with music, art, and cultural activities.

897   Go to the next **Dinosaur Time Trek** at Cal Expo and see larger-than-life dinosaurs, get more familiar with prehistoric poop, race through a prehistoric time labyrinth, and take the family Cretaceous Challenge.

898   Go to **Green Acres** nursery and see rows and rows of all the different types of plant varieties that can grow in Sacramento.

899 Get patio seating at **Rio City Café** on the river at sunset and watch the sky light up with bands of beautiful pastels.

900 Take a set of colored pencils to the River Walk and **sketch the tower bridge** and rushing river below it. Frame it and give it to a relative you love.

901 Play a round of golf at **William Land Golf Course**, where all kids under 18 play free. For little kids, book a tee time an hour before sunset and play the Hole 1, 2, 3 Loop for just $5, kids free. Bring your camera.

902 **Meet your city council representative** at their next public event and tell them what your family would like to see happen in your community.

903 Watch famous artists, scientists, writers, athletes, and public service veterans walk the red carpet outside the **California Museum** at the end of November for their annual California Hall of Fame inductee ceremony. Past inductees have included Oscar-Nominated Actor Harrison Ford (Han Solo) and Olympic Gold Medalist in Figure Skating, Kristi Yamaguchi.

904 Introduce the kids to **vinyl records** at Kicksville Vinyl & Vintage.

905   Join a nationally recognized singing ensemble at **Sacramento Youth Chorus**, part of the Sacramento Performing Arts Conservatory. Singers build friendships, cultural awareness, and get involved in the community. Ages 7-18.

906   Become a **Zoo Ambassador** and volunteer to help with events and projects at the Sacramento Zoo. Volunteers are needed every day of the week. Ages 15 & up.

907   Score points with older, comic-loving kids by suggesting the **Wizard World Sacramento Comic Con**. Act like you go all the time.

908   Look for the **fairy door** on a big tree next to the McKinley Park Rose Garden. Or make your very own fairy door on a tree at your favorite Sacramento park.

909   Do **swan dives** off the diving board at Davis Manor Pool.

910   **Rent a laminator** from Sacramento Public Library's "Library of Things" and make some bookmarks or calendars with family pictures for grandparents or family friends.

911   Grab a pole, dig for worms, and **fish for some bass or trout** at Mather Regional Park.

912   Share in the culture of Japan at the annual **Buddhist Church of Sacramento Bazaar**, held in August, where you can watch dramatic Taiko drummers, classical Japanese dancing, and eat traditional ramen, sushi, musubi, and bento.

913   Go to a **kids' cooking class**. **Sacramento Natural Foods Co-op** combines storytime with homemade snacks in the Kinder Cooks & Books program for ages 4 & up. Older kids can learn how to make Indian dishes, pasta dishes, and more. The Asian food market **99 Ranch** offers free impressively creative cooking classes for kids at their Sacramento and Folsom locations, inquire at the store to fill out enrollment forms. Ages 6-12.

914   In February, watch local kids take their **"hot jazz"** skills to the next level at the **Traditional Jazz Youth Band Festival**, packed with jazz clinics, mentored jam sessions, and non-competitive performances for youth bands and ensembles. Tickets to watch the evening performances are available to families and the general public: *sacjazzfoundation.org*. Students with I.D. get in free.

915   **Eat lunch in the middle of a plant nursery** on your way back from Tahoe at High-Hand Café in Loomis.

916   Shred it up (or just watch other kids take the fall) at one of the **top skate parks** in NorCal: 28th & B Skate Park, Granite Skate Park, McClatchy Skate Park, Tanzanite Skate Park, and Robertson Skate Park. Bring a helmet and knee/elbow pads.

917   **Grab a sword and try fencing**, an ancient sport which dates back to the 12th century, with a youth class at a fencing club, like Davis Fencing Academy, Premier Fencing Academy, or Sacramento Saber Fencing.

918   **Donate your outgrown winter clothing** to Lilliput Family Services, an organization that helps kids in foster care find their lifelong families. An older a child is, the more likely they will "age out" of the system without finding lifelong families. Twenty percent of kids who age out of the foster system at age 18 become instantly homeless and have greater risk for incarceration, even though 7 out of 10 kids in foster care say, if given the chance, they would like to pursue a college degree.

919   Join a kids **ensemble acting class** at Sacramento Theatre Company, held at Riverside United Methodist Church, and have fun becoming another character. Sessions culminate with a short play and/or monologue for family and friends.

920 Unleash your pen and enter the **Roseville Young Playwrights Festival** in November. Then enter your play in other festivals and writing contests. Don't be discouraged by setbacks. If you think you might want to be a writer, just keep writing!

921 **Get certified as a lifeguard** with a one-week course with the City of Sacramento. The Lifeguard Academy offers American Red Cross Training for kids 15-and-a-half & up. Must be able to swim 300 yards (12 laps) of front crawl and breaststroke, treat 2 minutes using only your legs, and swim 20 yards of front crawl and surface dive 10 feet to retrieve a 10-pound brick, place it on your chest, and return to the wall… in one minute and forty seconds.

922 See how many circular revolutions you can make with your body as you drop four stories into an open bowl on **The Vortex** ride at Golfland Sunsplash. Must be 48".

923 Go paddle boarding on the Sacramento River with **Sac SUPS**. Set-up a family lesson and just show up.

924 Pack a picnic and play a **game of hangman or bananagrams** on the green River Walk Park and promenade on the west bank of the Sacramento River, where you can get a **great view of the Ziggurat building,** the famous pyramid-shaped, terraced building. If you go close to sunset, you can see the golden Tower Bridge in all its brightest and shiniest.

925 **Brush up on the names of clouds** and which clouds are most common in Sacramento. Then find a big grassy field, lie down, and study them. *sactownkids. com/clouds*

926 Rent the **Intuos Pro graphics tablet** at the Arcade Public Library's "Library of Things," and doodle or illustrate something special using modern digital tools.

927 Spend a fun-filled night with scavenger hunts, crafts, a theater show, and bedtime stories at the **Family Campouts** during the summertime at Fairytale Town.

928   **Make your own pottery projects at home** and take it to Alpha Fired Arts to get fired. It's just $0.15 per cubic inch in most cases.

929   **Chart your next bike adventure** in Roseville. Get a free Roseville Parks, Trails, & Bikeways Map at the Downtown Roseville Library or Alternative Transportation Office.

930   In the spring and fall, take a **free tree tour** in a local Sacramento park with an expert at **The Sacramento Tree Foundation**. *sactree.com/treetours*

931   Drive a half-hour from Davis for the first sight of **Lake Berryessa** in Napa County and the formidable Monticello Dam.

932   Race down the snowy hill in a **tandem chute** at Hanson's Snow Tube and Saucer Hill in South Lake Tahoe near Heavenly Ski Resort.

933   Take an **equestrian lesson** at Gibson Ranch Regional Park, 325-acres of open countryside, and only 15 minutes from Sacramento.

934   **Learn by heart some jaw-dropping magic trick**s with Steve of Grand Illusions in Carmichael. One-hour classes are held on Saturday afternoons for kids ages 10 & up. Learn a different set of tricks every time.

935 Go to **SacBike.org and find maps and off-street paths** great for biking with children in and around Sacramento. Bike your way through a new park or neighborhood.

936 See and hear real **authors and writers speak** at the Sacramento Public Library. Go to the *saclibrary.org's* website and click on Events, then Authors & Speakers, for writers coming through town. Recommended for teens.

937 Escape the summer heat and go ice skating year-round at Roseville's **Skatetown.** Public skate hours daily.

938 Go to a Sacramento Public Library branch and find the newspaper on microfilm for **the day you were born**.

939 Let your thoughts and words flow at the **Wakamatsu Poetry Workshop** in a peaceful setting on a farm built in the 1800s in Placerville. Ages 8 & up. *arconservancy.com*

940 Blast to the past at **Burr's Fountain**, a charming old-fashioned diner and ice cream parlor in East Sacramento.

941 Dress up for **"High Tea in the Orchard"** at Harris Tree Farm in Pollock Pines in mid-summer. Register in advance.

942 See if you can see the **city skyline from atop the ferris wheel** at the Scandia Family Fun Center.

943 Bring your own bucket and clippers and pick your own flowers at the next u-pick flower event with **Flourish Farm West Sacramento Urban Farm**. $25 for a bucket of flowers.

944 Cross the **pedestrian-only Jim Jones Bridge** and listen to the water rush under your feet.

945 Flip around at an **open gym night**, like at Elevate Gymnastics Academy in Elk Grove on Saturdays. Many other Sacramento gymnastics schools open to the public on certain days, check their current schedules.

946 Hone your singing chops by taking a **musical theatre class** with Sacramento Showbiz through the city's recreation program. Open to all ages, but subject to teacher's approval before enrolling. *sacshowbiz.com*

947 Rev up your engines and go **indoor kart racing** at K1 Speed.

948 Teens can take part in the ever-growing **Sacramento Fashion Week** in the fall. Local designers and recent graduates from local academic institutions create a stunning showcase of their newest collections. Attend a free panel/forum to get a taste of the fashion industry's variety of careers.

949   Children with limited mobility or special needs can dance their hearts out with **Core Contemporary Dance's Adaptive Dance Program.**

950   Dance-lovers can **learn the waltz, salsa, and merengue** in the Children's Program at Capital Dance Center in Rancho Cordova. Discount trial classes for new young students. Ages 4-18.

951   **Walk a slinky** down the west-facing stairs inside the Capitol building, and other semi-inappropriate places.

952   Try a **family/group archery lesson** with Deborah's Mobile Archery Range. Deborah's a Level 2 Instructor with USA Archery, is great with kids, and can meet at Yolo Bowmen in Davis, Discovery Park in Sacramento, or El Dorado Hills Bowmen in El Dorado Hills. Don't have a bow or quivers? All equipment is provided.

953   **Write a letter to your state senator**, with your ideas to improve your neighborhood or community and drop it off at their office. Don't be surprised if they're there and want to meet you! Find out who represents your district at *findyourrep.legislature.ca.gov*

954   See and taste some unusual and colorful Asian varietal fruits and vegetables at the **Sacramento Asian Farmers Market**, on 5th St. & Broadway, just a block from the more popular Sunday Farmers Market under the freeway on 8th & W St.

955   Drop-in for an hour of unstructured gymnastics play for little ones during open gym at **Tumblebuddies**, and let them go wild on the zip line. Or plan ahead for a scheduled baby/toddler class.

956   **Read your favorite book to a dog** every first Tuesday of the month at Sacramento Public Library's "Read to a Dog" program. Therapy dogs are accompanied by Lend-A-Heart Association volunteers, and the dogs are cute and cuddly listeners. All ages and reading levels welcome. Bring a book or borrow one there. Check for the next "Read to a Dog" event at *saclibrary. org.*

957   Enter the world of coin collecting and **see Flying Eagle Cents from the 1800s**, Indian Cents, Half Cents, Early Dimes, and Small $1 Bank Notes from the 1920s at the **Excelsior Coin Gallery** on Arden Way. Recommend for older kids.

958   Turn yourself into any kooky character you can imagine at **Evangeline's Costume Mansion** in Old Town. Two floors in this historic building houses room after room of fun get-ups.

959   Camp lakeside very close to home at **Beals Point Campground** on Folsom Lake, at the start of the 32-mile Jedediah Smith Bike Trail. There are 57 camp spots near the water, with picnic tables, toilets, and showers.

960   View the river from breathtaking heights on the
Historic Fair Oaks Bridge, site of a few Hollywood
feature films.

961   Get a better grip on your backhand and serve with
family tennis lessons at McKinley Park with the City
of Sacramento recreation program (coach Ken Selby).
All levels, ages 4 & up.

962   Try cross-country skiing at **Tahoe XC's 24 groomed
trails** and 3 warming huts. A season pass for kids 12
& under is just $1. Dogs allowed too, for a... (ahem)...
slightly higher fee, $59.

963   Dive around a heated pool to find the perfect
Halloween pumpkin at the **Pumpkin Splash Patch**
at the community pool in El Dorado Hills. Decorating
supplies will be on-hand for creativity unleashed. Pre-
register at *eldoradohillscsd.org*. Ages 3-10, $12.

964   **Take your dog for some off-leash fun** on Pioneer
Park's five acres in Davis. (That is, dogs that respond
to commands and are not prone to running away with
the circus, of course.)

965   Celebrate Brazilian food, dance, and join in on some
kids' activities at the ever-colorful and vibrant
annual **Carnaval** in February at CLARA Studios.
braziliancentersac.org

966   Tour a valley oak riparian forest in **search of migratory songbirds** at the Regional San's Bufferlands' annual **Walk on the Wildside** event, a celebration of International Migratory Bird Day at Beach Lake Park in Freeport. See a rare heron and egret rookery, a collection of more than 120 active nests of great blue herons, great egrets, and double crested cormorants. Spotting scopes available for use. Free. *regionalsan.com/event/walk-wildside*

967   Become able to tell the differences between minerals, fossils, gems, and meteorites at the **Sacramento Mineral Society's** annual show in October. You'll find many people who will be delighted to talk about rocks.

968   Play **volleyball in the sand at Lake Forest Park** in El Dorado Hills. Use a big beach ball or balloon for little kids.

969   Celebrate **National Youth Art Month** in April by going to an art show at a nearby high school. Every year **Elk Grove Fine Arts Center** honors a different high school in their district by showcasing student artworks, which are always stunning and captivating – a peek into a teen's life experiences.

970   Cool off with a splash at the **Folsom Aquatic Center**. Twisty water slides and a great splash pool for toddlers make this an ideal summer destination for water-lovers.

971 Ride bikes through the big, old Oak trees along the Humbug Willow Creek Bike Trail and stop for a break at the **Folsom Kids Play Park**, or **"Castle Park"** as locals call it, and bumble around on some real wooden playground structures with super-giant tires, perfect for a game of hide-and-seek tag. Bring a bucket and shovel for a good dig in the sandbox.

972 Venture out to **Sailor Bar**, a versatile park once settled by gold-seeking sailors. Go rafting, fishing, horseback riding, or nature exploring. Riparian (riverside) habitats are teeming with wildlife. Look out for deer, coyotes, hawks, and owls.

973 **Introduce kids to the wonderful world of classical music**. Find out when the next celebrated concert pianist or world-class violinist is playing their way through the Mondavi Center in Davis. Especially for kids taking music lessons. Recent performers include world-famous violinist Itzhak Perlman.

974 Head down to **Autumn in the Park in Davis** in October, hosted by the Boy Scouts of America, and enjoy a scouting showcase, food, games, and a free outdoor movie for the kids.

975 Find buttercups and lupine **wildflowers at Lake Beach** on the north shore of Lake Tahoe in the summer. Follow directions to Skylandia State Park, then take Bristlecone Street to the very end.

976   Climb the outdoor playground, ride the carousel, run around the indoor playground, and ride the strangely smooth robotic animal rides (located in front of Sears) at the **Galleria at Roseville**. Swing by Fun Factory for some arcade fun.

977   Horseback ride along beautiful South Lake Tahoe at **Camp Richardson Corral** (ages 6 & up) or **Zephyr Cove Resort Stables** (ages 7 & up).

978   Watch traditional Italian folk dancers while slurping up some Italian pasta at the **Festa Italiana** in August. Try your hand at the salami toss, bocce games, craft activities, and more. Kids 15 & under free.

979   **Share a Romanian kürtőskalács**, a soft-serve-like ice cream in fluffy, churro-like doughnut cones (called chimney-cakes) at Sweet Dozen Cones in historic Folsom.

980   Sled down the white slopes in the little town of Strawberry at the **Kyburz Park n Play**, about an hour east of Sacramento on Highway 50. $10 parking. Stop in for some hot cocoa at the **Strawberry Lodge**.

981   Get all of your crafts supplies and ripped clothes together and enter the annual **Scarecrow Contest** in El Dorado Hills in October. Free.

982   Drop in for free admission to the **Roseville Utility Exploration Center**, a kid-friendly exhibit and exploration center to teach the next generation about waste, recycling, electricity, and water – our precious natural resource.

983   See some **strange and other-worldly succulents** at a succulent show, like the Sacramento Cactus & Succulent Society's Annual Show the first weekend in May. You'll get to see the best of the best by local growers.

984   Find a **free Taekwondo class** to train in self-discipline and self-respect, like at Robinson's Taekwondo or Family Taekwondo Plus.

985   Do some stick drills and learn rules of lacrosse at a youth camp like **Ryquin Lacrosse**, where even 3-7 year olds can participate in a co-ed league. There are leagues and camps in almost every Sacramento area.

986   Shop local for the next kid's birthday at the endlessly cute kids' boutique, **Moppet Shoppe** on J St. Then, re-stock your art supplies right across the street at **University Art**, which also stocks some great, art-focused kids books and gifts. Moms can pop their heads into **RIRE boutique** and **ShopCuffs** before calling it a day, since mom jeans are back in fashion.

987   Go to the **2nd Saturday Art Walk** and feast your eyes on the newest local art, 4pm-9pm. Invite family friends and make a night of it.

988   Get spooked by the **Sacramento History Museum's Ghost Tours** and hear about colorful characters in the Gold Rush days, and how they died. Runs in October only and recommended for ages 8 & up.

989   Get locked in a room and work as a team to escape within 60 minutes at the **Game Room Adventure Cafe**. Or enjoy hours worth of board games or join in on a game event. This popular Elk Grove spot is opening a new cafe in El Dorado Hills, complete with food, milkshakes, and craft sodas.

990   Go to a fast-moving **roller derby** by Sac City Rollers at The Rink. Watch teams with awesome names (like Capitol Punishers and Folsom Prison Bruisers) battle it out. You'll never look at roller skating the same way again.

991   Don a cowboy hat and **go to a local rodeo**, like the Folsom Pro Rodeo in July.

992   Become fluent in Spanish with kids and parent/tot classes at **Casa de Español.** Explore the worlds of pre-Columbian indigenous civilizations through art, food, and music at their enchanting 8-day summer camps.

993   Find out when Safetyville USA is hosting their next **Family Bike Night** and get your wheels pumped for the big event.

994   Celebrate the annual **fall migration of the Kokanee salmon** at the Fall Fish Festival at Taylor Creek near South Lake Tahoe.

995   **Practice your trigonometry** and compete in a Math League Competition with SACMATH at any grade level, elementary through high school.

996   Play **pick-up dodgeball** on Sunday Family Open (all ages) at 4pm at Olympus Sports Coliseum.

997   Go to the fantastic **Biodiversity Museum Day** in February. Get rare access to scientific collections and talk to UC Davis scientists and emeritus professors. Recent events have included: dinosaur bones in the Paleontology Collection, carnivorous plants at the Conservatory, and art and prehistoric tool demonstrations (like flint knapping, atlatl throwing) at Anthropology!

998   Join the free **Sacramento Kings Kids Club** for discounts on tickets and opportunities to participate in special Kids Club activities throughout the basketball season.

999   Go **star-gazing from a deep, dark sky** where
       astronomers do, at IHOP, or **Icehouse Observation
       Plateau**, in Pollock Pines.

1000   Get down for **Musical Robot**, the hilarious and
       energetic Auburn-based duo, Scott and Jason, who
       sling their little ukulele, drums, and accordion to
       toddler nirvana. Their album Wake Up Robot! Is
       available on iTunes, CDBaby, and Amazon. Find their
       next show at *musicalrobotlovesyou.com.*

1001   Just "play with your **friends** anywhere." This one was
       my 6-year old kid's idea. By far, the best idea.

101
DAYTRIPS

101 DAYTRIP (OR OVERNIGHT) IDEAS

A lazy Sunday can be a much-needed reprieve from the stresses of the week, but a couple times a month we like to venture out of bounds and see all the beauty, excitement, and abundance of learning opportunities that Northern California has to offer.

1. Visit the Lawrence Hall of Sciences atop the hills of **Berkeley**. Car picnic in the parking lot for some of the best views of San Francisco.

2. Drive out to **Muir Woods** and walk through a cathedral of Redwood trees.

3. Watch water burst into the air at **Old Faithful Geyser in Calistoga**. Bask in the mist and rainbows, then visit the sheep, llamas, and fainting goats.

4. See sea stars, sea anemones, and other organisms that live in subtidal nearshore habitats at the UC Davis **Bodega Marine Laboratory** near Bodega Bay. Free drop-in docent tours are available Fridays 2-4pm, check schedule for University holidays or other closures.

5. Visit **Glass Beach** in Mendocino and ride the **Skunk Train** through a redwood forest.

6. Let your imagination run wild at the Tech Museum of Innovation in **San Jose**.

7. Wander through a rainforest filled with butterflies at the Academy of Sciences in **San Francisco**.

8. Visit the San Francisco Model Yacht Club at **Spreckels Lake** in Golden Gate Park, and watch remote controlled boats coast on the water. Bring a picnic.

9. Take the **Urban Adventure Quest** for San Francisco (they have one for Sacramento too) and work as a team to figure out clues and puzzles, learning facts and history, visiting interesting places covering a couple of miles. Perfect for older kids.

10. Visit rescued animals at **Animal Place** in **Grass Valley**.

11. Get an early start and drive out to **Calaveras Big Trees State Park** to walk among giant redwoods.

12. Follow Mark Twain's travels through gold rush towns and find his famous jumping frogs in **Angels Camp**.

13. Take a 1 hour 45-minute **Amtrak train ride** to Oakland's Jack London Square for about $29 each way.

14. Go on a safari through 400 acres of wildlife preserve at Safari West in **Santa Rosa**.

15. Trek down to **Carmel Beach**, play on the fine white sand, and spot pelicans and sandpipers. Head south a few miles to **Point Lobos State Reserve** to see the sea lions at Sea Lion Point Trail. **Earthbound Farm in Carmel Valley**, the largest grower of organic produce in the world. Visit the organic kid's garden, aromatherapy labyrinth, and a cut-your-own-herbs garden. Check for special summer events. Best for overnight trips.

16. Tour a 13th-century style Tuscan Castle, complete with a moat, drawbridge, and dungeons at **Castello di Amorosa** in **Napa**.

17. Climb all over a quarter-scale railroad park at the **Sonoma Traintown Railroad**. Take a 20-minute train ride to the zoo where you can feed the animals.

18. Pack up the bikes (or rent them there) and bike along the **Truckee River Bike Trail** near Lake Tahoe.

19. Check out the **Bay Area Discovery Museum** near **Sausalito**, a kid-friendly favorite. Wander to the **Lookout Cove** for tide pools, shipwrecks, caves, and spider web installations.

20. Visit the **San Francisco Maritime National Historic Park**, where a three-mated cargo ship and paddle steamboat are docked. Take off your shoes at the nearby Aquatic Park, a sandy mini-beach that kids love.

21. Get a 360-degree view of **San Francisco** from the top of Coit Tower. There are elevators for kids.

22. Visit the Cable Car Museum in **San Francisco's Nob Hill**. Then ride the trolley through the city.

23. Walk 3.5 miles of white beaches at **Ocean Beach** in San Francisco. Look for the two windmills.

24. Take the ferry from **Vallejo** to San Francisco's Pier and visit the Exploratorium.

25. Swim in two geothermal mineral pools at **Morton's Warm Springs Resort** in **Glen Ellen**.

26. Explore scenic trails and beaches at **Point Reyes** National Seashore.

27. See the **Golden Gate Bridge** from the lush, green Crissy Field. Bring a picnic and a kite or frisbee.

28. Take a one-day tour of **Yosemite** with a tour company. Expect a 6am start time, a gorgeous ride on the San Joaquin Amtrak line, and a return departure time between 4:30-6:00 pm.

29. Scramble up rocks at Rock City in **Mount Diablo State Park**.

30. Visit the **Winchester House in San Jose**. The owner, Sarah Winchester, believed the house was haunted so she ordered continuous construction for almost 40 years until she died. Tour the 160-room mansion and the estate's elaborate gardens.

31. Hike part of the **Tahoe Rim Trail** at Lake Tahoe.

32. Venture out to **Empire Mine State Historic Park** in Grass Valley and see where gold seekers have mined more than 5 million ounces of gold.

33. Go hiking, swimming, and canoeing at **Lake Berryessa** near Napa Valley.

34. Go horseback riding at the beach at **Half Moon Bay** with Sea Horse Ranch (ages 5 & up). Then go tide pooling.

35. Ride the ferris wheel on the oceanside boardwalk in **Santa Cruz**.

36. Go to the annual **World Dog Surfing Championships in Pacifica** in August.

37. Watch the best surfers in the world compete at the **Titans of Mavericks** surfing competition in Half Moon Bay in January.

39. Spend the afternoon wandering around the **San Francisco Museum of Modern Art**. Kids under 18 are always free. Check out the exhibits kids especially love: *https://www.sfmoma.org/visit/visiting-with-kids/*

40. Fill a fun-filled day at **Golden Gate Park** in San Francisco. Roam through the Conservatory of Flowers, play at the Children's Playground (a.k.a. Koret Playground), row a boat at Stow Lake, and look for the buffaloes in the Bison Paddock.

41. Go to Family Sundays at the **Oakland Museum of California**. You can play their garden games or check out a book and picnic blanket at the Level 2 ticketing desk. Be sure to find the 9,000-pound Jade stone named Nephrite.

42. Brace yourselves and take a visit to **Alcatraz Island** and go on a tour of the former prison. Recommended for teens and older.

43. See the San Francisco Giants play a riveting game of baseball at **AT&T Park**.

44. Go canoeing down the **Russian River** in Napa.

45. Learn all about Jack London at the **Jack London State Historic Park in Glen Ellen**.

46. Take the ferry from Sausalito to **Tiburon** for a day of hiking, biking, and exploring. Hike up to the Old Saint Hillary's Open Preserve for wildflowers blooming around a 19th-century church in the springtime.

47. Take a picnic and your sand castle tools to **Stinson Beach** in the summertime and watch the fog roll in.

48. Hike through 600 acres of marshland at the **Pescadero Marsh Natural Preserve**. Birds migrate through this area during the early spring and fall months. Head down to Pescadero State Beach and look for mussels November through April. Check ahead for current conditions and closures.

49. Watch a chorus of more than 4,000 elephant seals at **Año Nuevo State Reserve** December through March.

50. Visit **Big Basin Redwoods State Park**, California's oldest state park, and one of the best places in the area to see old-growth redwoods.

51. Take your binoculars to **Point Montara Lighthouse** and look for gray whales in the winter and spring.

52. Get ready for some wild rides at California's Great America in **Santa Clara**, a theme park with thrilling roller coaster rides and water features.

53. Venture out to **Gilroy Gardens Family Theme Park**, a lush forested park with six different themed gardens, circus trees, and special family events.

54. Go to **Clear Lake**, California's largest natural lake, and one of the best bass fishing spots in the country.

55. Hike the 3.4-mile out-and-back **Tennessee Valley Trail** near Mill Valley for spectacular views and a stretch of beach at the end of the trail. Bring a picnic.

56. Watch a **Golden State Warriors** basketball game at Oracle Arena in Oakland.

57. Check out one of the deepest gold mines on the planet at Kennedy Gold Mine Tours in **Jackson**.

58. Explore the San Francisco bay on a boat cruise starting at **Fisherman's Wharf**, then get some hot chocolate at Ghirardelli Square.

59. Take teens on the **Ansel Adams Photo Walk** every Tuesday, Thursday, and Sunday in the summer, starting at the **Majestic Yosemite Hotel** at 9am. Free, but advance reservations required. Recommended for teens. *anseladams.com/camera-walk/*

60. See the **San Francisco Ballet** perform at the War Memorial Opera House, built in the 1930's and one of the last Beaux-Arts buildings built in the U.S.

61. Take the family for a lush winter hike on a small part of the **Rush Creek Open Space Preserve** in Marin County. Multi-use trails through green wetlands, nestled between hills, make for some stunning views.

62. Rent bikes and go for a bike ride through the picturesque **Squaw Valley** near Lake Tahoe.

63. Dance through wildflowers, climb atop Turtle Rock, and enjoy great bay area views at the **Ring Mountain Open Space Preserve** near Corte Madera.

64. Take a trip to **Children's Fairyland**, Oakland's Storybook Theme Park. Explore Lake Merritt and the surrounding area.

65. Go to the next Sleepover event at the **Monterey Bay Aquarium**. Look through one of the world's largest windows as they feed sharks, tuna, and other fish in the show-stopping Open Sea exhibit.

66. Explore the tunnels, lighthouse, and easy walking paths at the **Marin Headlands**. Stop by the Marine Mammals Center to learn about dangers to wildlife posed by humans and pollution.

67. Get lost in Egyptian history at the **Rosicrucian Egyptian Museum in San Jose**, modeled after the famous Temple of Amon at Karnak. See real mummies and don't miss the planetarium show every day at 2pm.

68. Run through secluded beaches, grassy fields, and enchanting forests at **Point Reyes National Seashore**.

69. Take a forest zipline above tree tops with **Sonoma Canopy Tours** (ages 10 & up).

70. Take a family horse ride through Del Monte Forest near **Pebble Beach** at Pebble Beach Equestrian Center. (Ages 7 & up, $95/person, 50 minutes.)

71. Go hiking at **Angel Island** and enjoy some of the best views of San Francisco. The island served as a war base during World War I and II, and also as an immigration station from 1910 to 1940.

72. Head south to the **Children's Museum of Stockton** and the **Pixie Woods Children's Park**.

73. Check out 580 glass prisms that make up the famous Fresnel lens at the **Point Sur Lightstation** at the free **Monterey Maritime Museum**.

74. Take the self-guided Botanic Interpretive Tour in the **Huckleberry Botanic Preserve near Oakland**, and discover unique plants that are found only in the Easy Bay.

75. Scream your lungs out at **Six Flags in Vallejo**.

76. Take a **sail on a boat around the San Francisco Bay**. Sometimes kids are free! (Example: Adventure Cat Sailing Charter prices: $45/adult, $25/kids 6-12, free for 5 & under)

77. Cook a gourmet kid-friendly meal at **CIA (Culinary Institute of America) at Copia in Napa** on Family Fundays.

78. Take a trip to the **Sacramento River Discovery Center** in the **Mendocino National Forest** about 2 1/2 hours away. The area around the center has been identified as one of the 200 most diverse ecosystems in the world.

79. Go to the **Presidio Visitors Center** in San Francisco and hop on the free PresidiGo shuttle to more than 40 destinations within the park, including 24 miles of trails.

80. Go hiking around **Fallen Leaf Lake** just south of Lake Tahoe. Swim, paddle, or raft in the summer.

81. Join **Sacramento Area Mushroomers** for $10/family and go on a mushroom identification hike. Past hikes have included Salt Point, Fleming Meadow, Sly Park, Shingle Springs, and Rockville Hills in Fairfield. *sacmush.com*

82. Rent bikes at the beginning of the **Camp Richardson Bike Path** and enjoy miles of family-friendly, paved trails along Lake Tahoe. Picnic at **Pope or Baldwin Beach**.

83. Play in a beautiful pool in the middle of a winery, splash in fountains, and play bocce ball at the **Francis Ford Coppola Winery in Geyersville** (all-day pool pass is $15-35, cabine package for four is $170). Inside the building is RUSTIC Italian restaurant, a tasting room, and a film gallery and memorabilia museum for all of Coppola's movies, including a real Academy Award.

84. Take young kids to **Sawmill Pond** near Lake Tahoe for some very gentle sledding in the winter.

85. Visit the **Sacramento National Wildlife Refuge** 90 miles north of Sacramento and explore shallow marshes and deep pond habitats. In the spring, shorebirds and songbirds abound on the 2-mile Wetlands Trail.

86. Find the **Pygmy Forest** off Airport Road in Little River in Mendocino County. Low, dwarfed cypress and redwood trees grew here as a result of rare ecological conditions involving underlying wave terraces and depleted nutrients in the soil. The trees may be 100 years old but they look like young saplings.

87. Go to San Francisco's **Treasure Island** for the San Francisco International Dragon Boat Festival, or just to spend the day.

88. Visit the **Mystery Spot** and find out why balls roll uphill in this strange house.

89. Hike Upper Eagle Falls in the springtime and see a little waterfall and big Lake Tahoe views of **Emerald Bay**.

90. Grab your lasso and high-tail it to at a dude ranch, like **Greenhorn Creek Guest Ranch in Quincy**, and live like a cowboy or cowgirl for a day. (Requires an overnight stay, and with the 3-hour drive you'll want to anyway.)

91. Take a **wildflower hike anywhere in the Tahoe Basin** in mid-spring. Go to *tahoesouth.com* for detailed wildflower trails.

92. Spend the afternoon in a Pop-Victorian British tea party wonderland at **Crown & Crumpet in San Francisco** and live like a Duchess for a day. Walk to the nearby Raymond Kimbell Playground or Alamo Square Park across from the cheerful Painted Ladies pastel-hued houses.

93. Visit the gargantuan, larger-than-life statues at **Wat Dhammararam Buddhist Temple in Stockton** during the Cambodian New Year Festival.

94. Go snowshoeing in the winter at **Donner Lake**.

95. Walk 2 easy miles of beautiful lakeside paths at Lake Tahoe's **Sugar Pine Point State Park**.

96. Explore D.L. Bliss State Park at Lake Tahoe, especially Calawee Cove and the short 1/2-mile **Balancing Rock Trail**.

97. Take a gondola ride up **Heavenly Mountain** at Lake Tahoe, or the aerial tram to High Camp in **Squaw Valley**. Don't miss the quaint Olympic Museum where you can stand on an Olympic podium.

98. Take a red **double-decker bus tour of San Francisco** and hop on-and-off at any point all day. Kids love it. Just remember to bring warm jackets with hoods or a snuggly hat.

99. Visit the **Walt Disney Family Museum** in San Francisco's Presidio. Then blow up a beach ball and play in the sand at nearby **Baker Beach**.

100. You can't officially tour the **Googleplex or Apple** in Silicon Valley, but you can get a glimpse of the campus and see the employees biking around on colorful bikes. You can also take pictures with their giant, quirky sculptures and drop by their nifty gift shops, open to the public. The nearby **Computer History Museum** has a self-driving car on display and is worth a visit. The Palo Alto Junior Museum and Zoo is also nearby.

101. Visit the Petrified Forest in **Calistoga** and see giant tree fossils that are an unfathomable 3.4 million years old. Famous horticulturist, Luther Burbank, donated a large piece of petrified wood from this forest to Central Park in New York City.

THE
ESSENTIALS

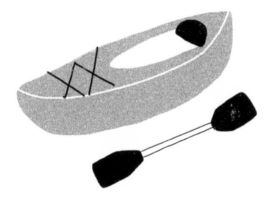

SACRAMENTO MUSEUM DIRECTORY

Aerospace Museum of California
aerospaceca.org
3200 Freedom Park Drive, McClellan, CA
916-643-3192
Hours: Tuesday - Sunday 10am - 4pm,
Closed on Monday. Free for 5 & under, 6-17 $8, Adults $10.

California Agriculture Museum
aghistory.org
1962 Hays Lane, Woodland, CA
530-666-9700
Hours: Tuesday - Saturday 10am - 4pm, Free for 5 & under,
6-12 $5, Adults $10.

California Automobile Museum
calautomuseum.org
2200 Front Street, Sacramento, CA
916-442-6802
Hours: Daily 10am - 5pm, Closed Tuesday, 3rd Thursday
10am - 8pm, Free for 4 & under, 5-17 $5, Adults $10.

California Museum
californiamuseum.org
1020 O Street, Sacramento, CA
916-653-7524
Hours: Tuesday - Saturday 10am - 12pm,
Sunday 12pm - 5pm; Closed Monday. Free for 5 & under, 6-17
$6.50, Adults $9.

California State Capitol Museum
capitolmuseum.ca.gov
Capitol Building, 10th & L Street, Sacramento, CA
916-324-0333
Hours: Daily 9am - 5pm. Free admission.

California State Library
library.ca.gov
914 Capitol Mall, Sacramento, CA
916-654-0261
Hours: Weekdays 9:30am - 4pm.
Free admission.

California State Railroad Museum
californiarailroad.museum
125 I Street, Sacramento, CA
916-323-9280
Hours: Daily 10am - 5pm, except major holidays.
Free for 5 & under, 6-17 $6, Adults $12.

California Statewide Museum Collections Center
www.parks.ca.gov
4940 Lang Avenue, McClellan, CA
916-263-0805
Hours: Tuesday 1pm - 4pm,
except major holidays.
Free admission.

Crocker Art Museum
crockerart.org
216 O Street, Sacramento, CA
916-808-7000
Hours: Tuesday - Sunday 10am - 5pm, Thursday 10am - 9pm.
Free for $6 & under, 7-17 $5, Adults $10.

Don & June Salvatori California Pharmacy Museum
cpha.com/about/foundation/salvatori-museum/
4030 Lennane Drive, Sacramento, CA
916-779-1410 ext. 326
Hours: Monday - Friday by appointment.
Free admission.

Fairytale Town
fairytaletown.org
3901 Land Park Dr, Sacramento, CA
916-808-7462
Hours: March – October, Daily 9am - 4pm (weather permitting); November – February, Thursday - Sunday 10am – 4pm (weather permitting). Check website for events. Weekday general admission $4.75, weekends $5.75, 2 & under free.

Folsom History Museum
folsomhistoricalsociety.org
823 Sutter St., Folsom, CA
916-985-2707
Hours: Tuesday – Sunday 11am - 4pm.
Free for 5 & under, 6-17 $4, Adults $10.

Leland Stanford Mansion State Historic Park
www.parks.ca.gov
800 N Street, Sacramento, CA
916-324-0575
Hours: Tours offered daily 10am - 5pm. Call for more info.

Maidu Museum & Historic Site
roseville.ca.us (search "maidu museum")
1970 Johnson Ranch Drive, Roseville, CA
916-774-5934
Hours: Monday - Thursday 9am - 4pm,
Saturday 9pm - 1pm, Third Saturday evening
6:30pm - 8:30pm, Closed Friday & Sunday. Free for 5 & under, Students $4, Adults $5, Family of Four $16, $2 after 2pm.

Museum of Medical History
ssvms.org/museum.aspx
5380 Elvas Ave, Sacramento, CA
916-456-3152
Hours: Monday - Friday 9am - 4pm,
Closed holidays. Free admission.

Old Sacramento Schoolhouse Museum
oldsacschoolhouse.scoe.net
1200 Front Street, Sacramento, CA
916-483-8818
Hours: Monday - Saturday 10am - 4pm,
Sunday 1pm – 4pm. Free admission.

Old Sacramento State Historic Park
www.parks.ca.gov
Front Street & I Street, Sacramento, CA
916-445-6645
Hours: Daily 10pm - 5pm. Free admission.

Powerhouse Science Center – Discovery Campus
powerhousesc.org
3615 Auburn Boulevard, Sacramento, CA
916-808-3942
Hours: Tuesday - Friday 12pm - 4:30pm;
Saturday - Sunday 10am - 4:30pm.
Free for 4 & under, 4-17 $7, Adults $8.

Roseville Utility Exploration Center
roseville.ca.us (search "exploration center")
1501 Pleasant Grove Blvd., Roseville, CA
916-746-1550
Hours: 10am - 5pm Monday through Thursday and Saturday;
Closed Friday and Sunday. Free admission.

Sacramento Children's Museum
sackids.org
2701 Prospect Park Drive, Rancho Cordova, CA
916-638-7225
Hours: Tuesday - Saturday 9am - 5pm; Sunday 12pm - 5pm. Free
for 1 & under, ; General Admission $8.50.

Sacramento History Museum
sachistorymuseum.org
101 I Street, Sacramento, CA
916-808-7059
Hours: Daily 10am - 5pm. Free for 5 &under,
6-17 $5, Adults $8.

Sacramento Zoo
saczoo.org
3930 W Land Park Dr, Sacramento, CA
916-808-5888
Hours: February to October, 9am - 5pm,
last admission at 4pm, November to
January, 10am - 5pm, last admission at 4pm.
Youth $7.75, Adults $11.75.

Sojourner Truth African American Museum
sojoartsmuseum.org
2251 Florin Road, Sacramento, CA
916-320-9573
Hours: Monday - Friday 8am - 4pm,
Saturday - Sunday 10am - 5:30pm (by appointment).
Free admission.

State Indian Museum
www.parks.ca.gov
2618 K Street, Sacramento, CA
916-324-0971
Hours: Daily 10am - 5pm. Free for 5 & under, 6-17 $3,
Adults $5.

Sutter's Fort State Historic Park
suttersfort.org
2701 L Street, Sacramento, CA
916-445-4422
Hours: Daily 10am - 5pm. Closed Thanksgiving, Christmas
and New Year's Day. Free for 4 & under, 5-17 $3, Adults $5.

Verge Center for the Arts
vergeart.com
625 S Street, Sacramento, CA
916-448-2985
Hours: Wednesday - Saturday 11am - 6pm; Sunday 12pm - 5pm. Closed Monday and Tuesday. Free admission.

Wells Fargo History Museum – Downtown
wellsfargohistory.com
400 Capitol Mall, Sacramento, CA
916-440-4161
Hours: Tuesday through Saturday 10am - 4pm. Free admission.

Wells Fargo History Museum – Old Sacramento
wellsfargohistory.com
1000 2nd Street, Sacramento, CA
916-440-4263
Hours: Daily 10am - 5pm. Free admission.

FAVORITE SACRAMENTO CITY PARKS

Capitol Park
13th & L Street, Sacramento
After a visit to the Capitol, the surrounding park is a must-run-around destination, after running up and down the west Capitol steps, of course. A Civil Warm Memorial Grove features trees that were brought in as saplings in 1897 from famous Civil War battlefields. A camellia grove, trout pond, and World Peace Rose Garden give the kids lots to take in. Download the Capitol Park Tree Booklet from capitolmuseum.ca.gov to have a tree-hunting adventure. Find the Moon Tree, a California coastal redwood that began its life as a seed that orbited the moon aboard the Apollo 14 mission.

Discovery Park
1600 Garden Hwy, Sacramento
With 302 acres of greenery to explore where the Sacramento and American rivers meet, you'll want to bring some bikes or scooters to maximize the experience. This park sits along the 32 miles of the Jedediah Smith Memorial Trail (aka American River Bike Trail) and has popular fishing spots and a large archery field.

Garcia Bend Park
7654 Pocket Road, Sacramento
This popular park in the Pocket-Greenhaven neighborhood is perfect for a lazy walk along the river before playing some tennis, soccer, or running around the playground.

McClatchy Park
3500 5th Avenue, Sacramento
An inventive, amusing playground with giant bucket of popcorn and ice cream cone. Two tennis courts, a water spray park, public pool, 9-hole disc golf course, basketball court, and concrete skate park make this a great Oak Park destination.

McKinley Park
601 Alhambra Blvd, Sacramento
A 32-acre park in East Sacramento with a cute and cozy
library, 8 tennis courts, a colorful playground, softball fields,
public pool, 1-mile jogging trail, newly renovated pond with
ducks and geese, and an enchanting rose garden that blooms
all summer and well into fall.

River Walk Park
651 2nd Street, West Sacramento
From Old Town or Crocker Art Museum, you can walk across
Tower Bridge to River Walk Park, and enjoy a paved trail on
the west bank of the Sacramento River. It's a fun trek to get
to the other side and watch boats float down the river. There
are interpretive signs detailing the wildlife that thrive in this
area.

Southside Park
2115 6th Street, Sacramento
A 20-acre urban downtown playground with a solar system
theme, lake with fishing piers, large sandbox, public pool,
tennis, and basketball courts.

William Land Regional Park
3800 Land Park Drive, Sacramento
A vast 166-acre park in the Land Park neighborhood with
wide, open spaces great for a picnic under a tree any time of
year. It includes kid-favorites Fairytale Town, Funderland,
and the Sacramento Zoo. Find the two lakes and "secret" rock
garden. The William Land Golf Course lets kids golf for free.

Need more park ideas?
Find complete information on all
226 parks in the city of Sacramento at:
https://www.cityofsacramento.org/ParksandRec/Parks

AWESOME NATURE CENTERS

Consumnes River Preserve
consumnes.org
13501 Franklin Blvd, Galt
916-684-2816

A bit of a drive, but a perfect day out in nature if you like wide open spaces, flat terrain, and easy walking hikes on over 11 miles of well-maintained paths. There's 50,000 acres of protected land that is home to Sandhill cranes, hawks, and Black-necked Stilts, butterflies, beavers, rabbits, you name it. Don't miss the annual Winter Bird Festival in January, and the Ducks in Scopes events where they set up telescopes to accommodate everyone, including toddlers. You can even paddle around in a kayak! Pick up a paddling map and brochure at the visitor's center. Free parking.

Hours: Weekends, and holidays 9am-5pm. Open during the weekday, but hours vary. Call ahead.

Pro Tip: Leave a couple sets of binoculars in the car for spontaneous nature walks in parks... or parking lots!

UC Davis Arboretum
http://arboretum.ucdavis.edu
There is no address; the gardens are spread out along the UC Davis campus in Davis. Be sure to download the Arboretum map before going or visit the Headquarters office beforehand at 448 La Rue Rd, Davis, 530-752-4880

Sixteen gardens with specialty flowers and trees from all over the globe sits along a creek, with a 3.5-mile paved path for bikes and strollers. The grassy area at the west end of Peter Shield Grove is a perfect spot for picnics, games, and freeze tag. Download the visitor's map online or visit the Arboretum Headquarters. Check the calendar for special events like Jam Sessions, Botanic Fanatics, and Crafts and Cocoa. Free. Parking is free on weekends, $9 on weekdays.

Hours: Accessible all day, every day. Headquarters office hours are Monday through Friday, 8am-5pm.

Effie Yeaw Nature Center
sacnaturecenter.net
2850 San Lorenzo Way, Carmichael
916-489-4918

A nature preserve on 100 acres set along the American River.
Stop by the museum store to grab a map and get going on an
easy adventure hike to find deer, songbirds, woodpeckers,
jack rabbits, turkeys, frogs, and owls in their natural
environments: riparian and oak woodlands, shrub lands,
meadows, and aquatic habitats. Picnic under the live oak
tree next to the Maidu village. Check calendar listings for
family nature walks, events, and storytimes. Free, suggested
donation, $5 parking.

Hours: February through October, Open Tuesday through
Sunday: from 9am-5pm. November through January, Open
Tuesday through Sunday: from 9am-4pm. Closed on Mondays,
Open on Mondays that are public holidays, except Christmas
Day and New Year's Day.

Placer Nature Center
placernaturecenter.org
3700 Christian Valley Rd, Auburn
530-878-6053

Sixty acres of pure nature bliss for kids, with a windy 1-mile
trail through oak woodlands. An outdoor garden with
composting exhibits, Garrison's Park Nature Playscape,
Native American exhibit, and Discover Room will keep little
hands and feet busy for hours. Bring a lunch, there's plenty of
shade. Check calendar listings for events. Free parking.

Hours: Hours vary, call ahead or check online. Sometimes
only open on 2nd Saturdays in the Winter, November through
March. Free admission, fees for programs vary, check website.

ABOUT THE AUTHOR

Sabrina Nishijima is a stay-at-home mom and writer who lives in Sacramento with her husband, two kids, and their three-legged dog. Her favorite things to do with her kids are: picking oranges from their orange tree, looking for worms at night with headlamps (#647), sailing at Lake Natoma (#2), hiking in wildflowers (#975), learning new magic tricks (#858), and peering out into the universe from the Community Observatory in Placerville (#3). She has a passion for finding new adventures for her kids. Her previous work has been nominated for two Independent Press Association Awards, and has been published in Redbook, Glamour, Ladies' Home Journal, Girl's Life, Utne Reader, etc. This is her first book.

Get more fun adventure ideas at: **SACTOWNKIDS.COM**
Connect on Instagram: @sactownkids
Twitter: @sactownkids
Find us on Facebook: facebook.com/sactownkidsonline
Download the Sactown Kids app in the Apple Store or Google Play.

Sarah Golden is an artist living in Oak Park with her husband, twin girls, and beloved Boston terrier, Captain.

See and buy her artwork at: **SARAHGOLDEN.ORG**
Follow her on Instagram: @sarahgoldenart

WE HOPE YOU LOVE THIS BOOK!

TO ORDER MORE COPIES:

1. Visit your nearest **independent bookstore**.
Call ahead to ask if they have copies in-stock.
If they don't carry it, you can request it!
Support our local, indie bookstores!

2. Order at **SactownKids.com**.
Get a free bookbag with your order! *(Limited time)*

3. Order online at **Amazon.com**,
BarnesandNoble.com, or **IndieBound.org**.

Don't forget to sign-up for our newsletter at
SACTOWNKIDS.COM

Get tons of new ideas for new adventures in Sacramento for ages 0-101, plus weekly e-mails or texts of our Top 20 things to do with kids (and the young at heart) in Sacramento.

Get out and try something new!

Download our free app in the Apple Store or Google Play Store and plan adventures on the fly!

Comments, Suggestions, Tips?
Is your favorite thing to do in Sacramento *not* in this book?
Write us at hello@sactownkids.com, or connect
with us on Instagram or Facebook!

Independent Bookstores in Sacramento

Avid Reader at Broadway Station
1945 Broadway, (916) 441-4400
Beers Book Center
915 S St, (916) 442-9475
Book Collector
1008 24th St, (916) 442-9295
Carol's Books
1913 Del Paso Blvd, (916) 285-5191
Dimple Books & Vinyl on Arden
2499 Arden Way, (916) 239-3760
Dimple Books & Vinyl on Broadway
1600 Broadway, (916) 239-3750
The Hornet Bookstore
6000 J St, (916) 278-6446
J Crawford's Books
5301 Freeport Blvd #200, (916) 731-8001
Richard L Press Fine Books
1831 F St A, (916) 447-3413
Time-Tested Books,
1114 21st St, (916) 447-5696
Underground Books
2814 35th St, (916) 737-3333

(Note: Some stores may only sell used books, but it doesn't hurt to ask!)

TO ORDER AT A BULK DISCOUNT:

For gifts, clients, schools, fundraisers, educational programs,
reunions, baby showers, retirement parties, or meet-ups:

Order 10, get 30% off ($11.86)
Order 25, get 40% off ($10.17)
Order 100, get 50% off ($8.47)

For bulk orders, contact us at: hello@sactownkids.com

IDEAS & NOTES